Sacred
Suffering

Nancy Brandon
Editor

PROCLAIM PRESS

Some chapters of this book contain names and identifying details which have been changed to protect the privacy of the individuals involved. All events described are the personal remembrances of the chapter authors. Each chapter author is solely responsible for the content of their chapter.

Cover design by Jonas Barber, Barberhaus Design Studios
714.296.0861 www.barberhaus.com

"I have told you all this so that you may have peace in me. Here on earth you will have many trials and sorrows. But, take heart, because I have overcome the world."

Jesus

John 16:33 (NLT)

"The most beautiful people we have known are those who have known defeat, known suffering, known struggle, known loss and have found their way out of the depths. These persons have an appreciation, a sensitivity and an understanding of life that fills them with compassion, gentleness and a deep loving concern. Beautiful people do not just happen."

Elisabeth Kübler-Ross

CONTENTS

Dear Readers,

The stories you read in the following pages may raise questions or comments in your heart and mind. We want to hear your heart. Please visit **www.sacredsuffering.com** and click on "Contact Us" to communicate with us. Your comments will be read and when appropriate, responded to.

The web site will offer further resources for understanding and handling many kinds of suffering. This is also the place where you can contact the chapter authors.

The Publisher,
Proclaim Press

INTRODUCTION

Welcome to Sacred Suffering, an invitation to dialogue about the tough places in life.

This book is written for two kinds of people. It is for those who are watching their loved ones endure suffering and who want to understand or even encourage those they care about.

It is also for those who either have been or who are suffering. If this is you, then Sacred Suffering is a conversation with those who have been where you are. Through their stories they will show you how they survived, no, even thrived, through physical, mental, spiritual or emotional pain.

Some may ask whether there could possibly be any connection between what is sacred, that which involves God and suffering, that which involves pain.

My answer is the same as what Christian author, C.S. Lewis, said: "Pain insists upon being attended to. God whispers to us in our pleasures, speaks in our consciences, but shouts in our pains. It is his megaphone to rouse a deaf world."[1]

Not only can pain and suffering be God's way of getting our attention, it may be what He is using to form us into the people He created us to be. It also gets us to ask those really important life questions that need to be asked.

How do I know this?

I have lived it.

My grandmother was the first person I felt deeply connected to

---

[1] C. S. Lewis, *The Problem of Pain* (New York: Macmillan, 1962), 93.

who suffered and died from cancer. A few years later, my mother had breast cancer and then ovarian cancer before she died. Ten years later my younger brother was diagnosed, at the age of 31, with brain cancer. Another five years passed and two of my sisters' husbands, both in their forties, were given painful diagnoses, one of liver cancer and the other esophageal. All these family members died after suffering through surgeries and treatments that lasted from three months to two years. Each of their experiences caused me to ponder the "Why?" Eventually I asked the "what" question. "What are Your purposes in allowing these kinds of suffering, Lord?"

In 2000, I met Ginger, a special woman who was diagnosed with breast cancer at the age of forty. We became best friends. In the seven years before she died I had the opportunity to share in her experience and observe the way it changed her. I heard Ginger say, more than once, that as much as she struggled with the difficulties associated with her disease, she was grateful because she knew if it hadn't happened she would never have come to know Jesus and His love, grace and power in her life.

Three months after Ginger passed, in December of 2007, I was diagnosed with ovarian cancer. I hadn't yet thought of writing this book, perhaps because my surgery and five and a half months of chemo really wasn't so bad. At the end of the treatment I completed the last class requirement in my undergraduate bachelors of psychology degree and a few months later, began a Master's degree at Talbot Seminary in Spiritual Formation and Soul Care. Much of the program called for deep introspection with the Lord. We were required to open ourselves to the deep places of pain that dwell in all of our hearts. That is when the idea of this book began to take shape. I knew the title was to be *Sacred Suffering*, but that was all.

During that time another one of my brothers, who had suffered many years with a number of health problems, died suddenly from a heart attack. I was attending one of those classes that required us, in prayer, to open the deep places of our hearts to the Lord. That class and my brother's death triggered a surfacing of feelings and experiences I hadn't dealt with in many years.

In the midst of my grief over my brother's death, I had a conflict with a daughter that caused more pain (emotional pain that I also felt in my body) and suffering than I experienced in my cancer treatment. The conflict affected my marriage too. I recall telling someone that it was much easier for me to go through cancer treatment than to deal with the kind of pain brought on by that family emotional crisis. The conflict and tension drove us to seek out counseling. Eventually, the Lord allowed me and my family to heal and my husband and I to enjoy a greater depth and intimacy in our relationship than I thought possible. It was all as a result of the conflict and subsequent counseling we went through.

I am still so grateful that healing had occurred before another family crisis hit. My 91 year old father, an extraordinarily kind, wise and faithful man had to be placed in a skilled nursing facility while going through the end stages of congestive heart failure. It was painful to watch. My siblings and I committed ourselves to staying with him 24/7 as the facility was overcrowded and understaffed. Eventually we hired an overnight caregiver as we were all spent but not willing to leave him alone. Each of us took several "shifts" a week with Dad. Those shifts turned out to be tremendous blessings for Dad and for us, but also painful as we watched him truly suffer, physically, mentally and emotionally, as he lost his ability to do anything for himself and had to endure the humiliation of having people change his diapers and many other tasks. Hard, deep suffering.

After about three months in the facility, Dad passed away at 11:00 p.m. on a March evening, St. Patty's Day, 2012. God gave him the gift of being surrounded by his family as he drew his last breath. I was blessed to watch him pass from this world into eternity with Christ. Being with him during that season of suffering, I was able to observe what it looks like for one Godly man to suffer faithfully.

In the months after Dad died, while in the midst of my grief, the *Sacred Suffering* book kept coming to mind. I realized by then that I wasn't going to write the book on my own. Not only was God making it clear to me that He would be with me, but He was calling me to gather a group of strong Christian women who had endured seasons of various types of suffering in their lives. He began to assemble that group. Emails went out as I realized how many extraordinary women I knew and admired, who had journeyed through all kinds of painful circumstances. I asked each of them to write a chapter describing what it was like, both internally and externally, to walk through their time of suffering. At that point I wasn't sure I would be writing a chapter; I didn't believe I had experienced the deep kind of suffering that could give me the perspective I would need, but I knew these other women had, so I scheduled our first meeting for July, a couple of months down the road.

Two months after my dad passed, May 8th, I was just walking out of my last class of the semester when I turned my phone on to find that my family had desperately been trying to reach me. My son, living in Santa Rosa, a good nine hours from where I lived in Orange County, had a perforated colon and needed emergency life-saving surgery. My sister and I were on the road in less than an hour and arrived at the hospital just as Phil was being wheeled to his room. I saw my son suffering from excruciatingly painful procedures that would continue for weeks and my mother's heart felt as though it was being twisted and tortured in my chest as I watched. Although Phil's suffering was primarily physical and mine, emotional, I realized then that body pain affects the emotions and the spirit and that emotional pain touches the body and the spirit.

Toward the end of June, a week after we brought Phil back down to our house to complete his recovery, I got word that my cancer was back after a four and a half year remission.

That's when I came to ask of the Lord, "How? How do people, especially those who genuinely love and serve Jesus, as my dad did, how do they do this suffering thing?"

I have come to believe that the best way to answer the "How?" question is to listen to the stories of people who have done it and to learn from their example.

That is why I invite you to open your hearts to the stories of thirteen women who've journeyed through painful seasons of life. Their tales cover a wide gamut of situations. Here you will find suffering that ranges from widowhood, cancer, rape, abortion, addiction, divorce, the death of or catastrophic trauma in the life of their child to the painful grief over dreams not realized.

These daughters of the God of the universe have laid their hearts bare for one reason. They want you to find strength, encouragement, inspiration and insights in the midst of your own or a loved one's suffering.

So come along with these women who Jesus called to share their journey through suffering. Then, Lord willing, we will all be able to say what Job, in the Bible, said to God, "My ears had heard of you but now my eyes have seen you" (Job 42:5).

Nancy

Trish

Dear brothers and sisters, when troubles come your way, consider it an opportunity for great joy. For you know that when your faith is tested, your endurance has a chance to grow. So let it grow, for when your endurance is fully developed, you will be perfect and complete, needing nothing. If you need wisdom, ask our generous God and he will give it to you. He will not rebuke you for asking.   James 1:2-5 (NLT)

Consider it pure joy, my brothers and sisters, whenever you face trials of many kinds.... What? For me, that line from James 1:2 is one of those examples of how God does not always make sense. Wayne, my husband, used to upset me when he would thank God for the problems in our lives. I sometimes questioned him about those thankful prayers. I did NOT wish to have the trials we faced. He would gently remind me that God has a plan to use our trials. In my head I could understand, but my heart wanted to have words with the Lord. Frankly, I was not happy.

The James passage goes on to explain that these trials test our faith and produce perseverance and when our perseverance is allowed to grow, then we are mature and complete—ready for anything. In verse five, we are told that if we lack wisdom, we should ask God for it and He will generously give it to us.

What I couldn't understand then, I now have understanding about. I ask God for wisdom nearly every day—several times a day.

My suffering has matured me and prepared me for the path that the Lord already laid down for me.

I have begun to call my suffering a ministry of pain. Suffering has equipped me to reach out to others in ways that could have never happened without the pain. And helping others brings me great JOY! Thank you, Jesus. Only the Lord could turn something so dark and painful into something so beautiful.

I have been struggling with where to begin because there is so much. I guess it began when I was young and my parents got divorced. That was a very painful experience for me at a tender time in my life: junior high. My self-concept was compromised and it left me with anxiety that continued through my early adulthood. I suffered from panic attacks that had me calling doctors to see if I was having a heart attack.

Then, when I was married at age twenty-five, all the adjustments were too much for someone who just liked pleasing people. For a couple of years, I went to counseling and then continued my path of understanding through journaling my prayers and memories. I learned that developing myself into the person the Lord wanted me to be allowed my anxieties to decrease. I learned to speak up for myself and set better boundaries—sometimes I spoke up way too much.

When Wayne and I decided to start a family, the next hurdle race began. Every month, I faced so much pain when I wasn't pregnant. During our five year trial, several times I became pregnant, only to miscarry. After a D and C procedure, I became sick with contracted pneumonia. For the better part of a week, I just laid and rocked back and forth. My husband couldn't understand my emotions. He was sad, but I was broken. Tears fill my eyes as I write this, just remembering that sadness. Because I couldn't have children, I went to graduate school and completed my Masters of Social Work.

We began the process of adoption. We found a young lady who was pregnant and wanted us to adopt her baby girl. While she was pregnant, we took care of her and her three other children. We prepared for this baby. One day she showed us all of these pictures of her as a baby and the ultrasound pictures of the unborn little girl. I was so excited, but that night she stole all of our baby items and left. I was heart-broken. Why did she do that to us?

After some time, we found another birth mother and adopted baby Miles. We helped deliver him. We loved him. He had been exposed prenatally to substances, according to the birthfather. Poor

Miles had lots of his own personal trials throughout his life as a result of his own experiences. Even so, he is such a joy.

When Miles was four months old, doctors discovered and treated my previously undiagnosed thyroid condition. Then a surprise happened. I became pregnant with Evan. I was so scared it wouldn't last, but it did. I couldn't believe I had my own biological child. I was so happy. Miles was happy with his new baby brother. Life was great. I got pregnant again with Austin three and a half years later. Life was about as good as it got. We were very busy with three very young boys.

Flashing back to my time as a student, we purchased our first home in Long Beach, California. At the time we purchased our home, real estate prices in Southern California were increasing dramatically, so we thought we should buy before we were completely unable to do so. We planned to grow the equity and move in a year or so—or so we thought. We bought a home that we could afford. It was cute. It was built in 1906. We thought it was great, until the first night we stayed in our home.

All night long, in front of our home, which was on a corner, the ladies of the night would sing the blues, literally. The drug users and dealers used our corner to do their business because it was a good location to watch for approaching police. The gangs shot their guns every single night. We had to get a phone with a lighted keypad on it so we would not have to turn the lights on to call 9-1-1. We didn't sleep that first night. We were terrified. The second night we actually got a hotel room so we could sleep. We both grew up in quiet neighborhoods in Orange County and had no idea what a bad neighborhood looked like. It felt like we made the biggest mistake of our lives. But we made the best of it. We began to minister to the neighbors, the hookers and some of the gang bangers.

One day, after a long day at work, I was walking up to my front door and noticed a gang of teens on the street beating up another boy. I became so outraged that I marched right up to them in my high heels and dress and demanded that they release that boy. I think I almost died that day, but God spared me. Later, I realized that they were jumping that boy into a gang. Those kids glared at me and I glared back. They finally backed down, but were calling me all kinds of names. I was naïve, but I did what I felt compelled to do at the time. That got an ugly and scary ball rolling.

The gangs retaliated, which is what they do. Wayne was working in the yard one afternoon and someone came by and shot at him. They missed, as usual, because they were horrible shots, thank God! When we made the "mistake" of calling the police, it was like we declared war on them. One day, while Wayne was in the shower, one of the girls in the gang came to the door (we had a security door in place, which I kept locked) and asked if Wayne was home. I peeked out the side window and spotted a young man holding a gun. I lied and told the girl that Wayne wasn't home. She was flustered and said, "Okay" and left. We decided we had to move out right away. We went to stay with my mom until our home would sell, which took two years and we lost quite a bit of money. I didn't care. I was SO glad to get rid of that home.

In 1999, the real trials began. Wayne had just landed a full time position teaching math in a local junior high school. He had switched careers from architecture to teaching. He noticed that while at the chalk board he would sometimes become confused, feeling silly in front of the kids. Other times he would stumble while he walked. He was afraid people would think he had been drinking. His personality began to change. He was moody and depressed. We sought help from doctors, therapists and pastors, but nothing helped.

Even during this stressful time, my dear husband was always sweet and loving to me. One evening, he kissed my hand, called me "Cara Mia," (one of his many pet names for me) and began to slow dance with me to Andrea Bocelli's song, "Con Te Partiro." It was one of many sweet moments that I will carry in my heart for eternity.

The year prior to Wayne's death, we were fortunate to receive a big enough tax refund that we were able to travel as a family to Hawaii. It was a time to develop fun memories for the entire family, while Wayne still had enough strength. He needed to rest frequently, but was able to participate in most of the activities. I will never forget the road to Hana on the island of Maui. It was a very curvy drive. All three of my boys got carsick. I smile at that now, but wasn't smiling then. I also remember driving to the top of Haleakala—a dormant volcano, over 10,000 feet high. We had a couple of hours before we needed to arrive at the airport for our departure and I wanted to squeeze every experience I could into our little remaining time on the island. It was so beautiful, peaceful and quiet. The peak of the volcano was above the clouds. It was as if we were looking down from heaven. We watched the sun set from that vantage point. When we were leaving and still at the top of the volcano, my gas light went on. There were no gas stations anywhere near us. I prayed, put the car in neutral and coasted all the way down the mountain. I pulled into the airport, car still running and ready to leave. Whew! I will never forget that trip to paradise with my boys and my wonderful husband.

We looked for opportunities to build memories and to have fun. In the late summer, our extended family went camping. Austin was two years old. We decided to go out on the lake and to keep Austin at the campsite with my sister, since he was so young. After we left, Austin threw a tantrum because he was not allowed to go. He went too near the still smoldering campfire and stumbled and fell into it. My sister grabbed him and doused him with water. She sent for someone to find us on the lake and then she rushed him to the local hospital. Big Bear Lake is no small lake. I had no idea what was happening. We were trying to fish when all of a sudden some strange man came up to us in his boat and simply said, "Someone got burned at the camp," and then left.

I thought it was strange that this man would come up to us and tell us how someone got burned and leave so quickly. Then it hit me like a ton of bricks, which I believe was knowledge that the Lord gave me. I yelled, "Austin is burned!" We got back to shore as soon as we could and I ran all the way to camp. I asked the people in the next campsite and they told me that my sister took my son to the hospital. I had no idea how badly he might be burned. We prayed all the way there.

When we arrived, I found him by listening to the wails of my sister. He sustained minor burns on his back, but had third degree burns on his hand. It could have been so much worse. He was hospitalized for two weeks and had several surgeries. Wayne and I took turns staying with him. I worked during the day, dropped off the kids at a sitter and relieved Wayne while he worked at night. He would come back to the hospital and I would pick up the two boys and get them to bed. I would go off to work the next morning and we started the routine again until he was released. It was so hard to see my baby suffer.

All of these trials seemed to be progressively more difficult. I became tougher and stronger at each point in the journey, just like it said in James.

Two months later, the biggest trial began. Wayne was up on a ladder, trimming our olive tree. He came down for a break and noticed our next door neighbor fiddling with stuff in his garage. Wayne went over there and began to help him out. I joined him. The boys were there, too. Within a minute or two, Wayne began to stutter. Then he fell over. I realized he was having a grand mal seizure. While my neighbors tended to Wayne, I ran and called 9-1-1. My neighbor Carol was a flight attendant and had some training with seizure—thank God. The boys and I were stunned.

Two days later we found out that he had a mass in his brain. Within the week he had brain surgery and doctors determined that he had malignant brain cancer—the kind you die from. I couldn't eat for two weeks and lost fourteen pounds. Unless God healed him, my dear husband and father of my three little boys was going to die. I felt that I could crawl out of my skin. I wanted to die myself. If it weren't for my boys that still needed a healthy parent, I might have.

I entered into the hardest time of my life. So many times, I just threw my hands up into the air and told God that He needed to grab my hands and lead me, because I didn't know what to do and didn't have the strength to go on anymore. Wayne could no longer work. I had to work and care for my boys and my very ill husband. Again, I have tears in my eyes as I write these recollections. It was so exhausting; so much pain. But the weirdest thing was that while I was in my greatest pain, I was simultaneously experiencing my greatest joy. That is just so incredibly strange. I came to understand on a very personal level how God is, in fact, close to the broken-hearted.

Now let me tell you how God was close to me. He walked through this with me and sustained me. He strengthened me and gave me purpose, even while "in the valley of the shadow of death."

A few months prior, before we had any suspicion that Wayne was ill, the Lord put it on my heart to purchase life insurance. When I had previously asked Wayne about purchasing life insurance, he always put me off and said we needed to pay other bills first. This time I didn't ask. I just knew to do it. He didn't object when I told him that I set up the physical exam for the insurance. God put that on my heart. This insurance allowed me to stay home with the boys for a year after Wayne's death. Prior to his death, we still had financial concerns and we learned that God is big enough to handle these concerns.

Wayne had his first seizure two days after Thanksgiving. On December 5th, he had his brain surgery. He was in and out of the hospital a couple of times before Christmas. I hadn't the time, money, nor the energy to buy Christmas presents for my three small boys. Christmas was a magical time for my boys and it would be extra painful for us all to not have a Christmas that year. While I was visiting my husband at St. Jude Hospital one day, a nurse pulled me aside and informed me that the entire staff chooses one family each year to sponsor at Christmastime. We were the chosen family. We were so incredibly lavished with gifts that on Christmas morning, Evan took one look at the room filled with presents, dropped to his knees, clasped his hands together and loudly said, "God bless Santa!" During the midst of such painful turmoil, we felt so blessed and cared for.

One day, I realized that I was going to have to request a leave of absence from work and I didn't know for how long. I just knew that Wayne's needs were increasing and I needed to be the one to care for him. While I was driving to work, I prayed out loud to the Lord and said, "God, you own the cattle on a thousand hills. I need you to sell some of the cattle and give me the money so I can take care of our household expenses." God was happy to help.

I was off work for more than eight months with no income. God provided so beautifully that all bills were paid and debts were paid off. People just gave us money. One day I was at the grocery store and while I shopped I told God that I was spending the rest of the money and I needed more. Fifteen minutes later, I was home and saw a Federal Express envelope at the door. I ripped open the package, pulled out the contents and stared in disbelief. It was a check for $6000!!!

During the last few months of Wayne's life, it became necessary for Wayne to be placed into a nursing facility. It was too difficult to take care of him and I didn't want the boys to be exposed to Wayne's increased agitation. We did not have long term care insurance, but I knew I needed to still search for help. I began looking at more affordable places, like sharing a room with very old men. Wayne was only forty-four years old. He was very agitated all the time then. His care needs were very different from someone who was merely elderly. He needed a private room.

I found a place that was perfect. It was close to home and had a private room available. I spoke with the head nurse. She was very sympathetic, but said, "I have been doing this for twenty-five years and there is no way Wayne could be placed here."

I felt boldness build in me. I proclaimed to her, "Wayne will be here and God will pay for every dime." I still can't believe the boldness I had—it came from the Lord.

Within a few days, I received a call from our healthcare providers. They discussed our case and decided they would allow Wayne to be placed there. He was there for the last three months of his life and I never paid a dime! God is good. Our little boys and our dog could hang out with him, without disturbing any roommates. My husband had good care and felt peace.

One day, the nursing facility called me and told me that Wayne just had a really bad seizure and I needed to get there right away. I told them I would. The only problem was that my three little boys were home too. I didn't really have the time to find a sitter and wait for her arrival. I told the Lord that I needed Him to get me a sitter right away. While this was happening, the boy's former preschool teacher from church was driving near my home and felt an overwhelming urge to pull the car over and call me. She did, but as she was dialing, she heard in her head to just hang up and go to my house. Within minutes, their teacher was in front of my house telling me that she was supposed to babysit my kids. Unbelievable. God is good.

At one point our hospice workers (who were the best) explained to us that Wayne would eventually slip into a coma and then die. I understood them to say that many people wait and die when they are alone. That made me sad. I asked Wayne if he wanted me with him when he died. He said yes, so we prayed that we would be together when he went to be with Jesus. Praise God, he never went into a coma. Apparently, that is rare when you have a large brain tumor. I was by his side. He turned and looked straight into my eyes with his piercing blue eyes and then he turned and looked at someone else. I am sure it was Jesus. Then he was gone. It was a beautiful, sacred and tremendously sad moment, all rolled into one.

The night of his death felt particularly lonely and sad. Before I fell asleep, I was laying on my side, praying. Suddenly, I felt someone rubbing my back, exactly the way Wayne used to rub my back. I was startled and turned to see who was in my room with me. No one was there. I knew that the Lord had allowed a final gesture of comfort to let me know that I was not alone in my pain.

One night I asked Jesus to allow me to know how Wayne was doing in Heaven. In my spirit, I heard Wayne's voice tell me, "I am happier than you could ever imagine on earth." I felt great peace and had knowledge that one day I too would experience what he spoke of.

Now let me tell of a few stories that happened prior to his death. A few times that while I or someone else was praying for Wayne, God gave me messages. Once, while the elders came and prayed over Wayne, I heard the Lord speak to my spirit that Wayne's healing was already going to happen—in heaven. The healing on earth would take place in me. Another time, while Wayne was lying next to me in bed sleeping, I put my hand on his head, where the tumor was and prayed for his healing. The place in my own head become hot and again I received the message that the healing would be in me. It was strange. I wasn't sick. Another time I was talking to the Lord and telling him that this pain is just too much to bear. I heard the Lord speak word for word to my spirit. He told me, "*The pain you experience in this life is not significant, except for how it impacts eternity.*" That actually made sense to me and gave me a sense of purpose. I knew that God would use this pain to expand His kingdom and influence the world around me for the good.

When I cry my eyes get swollen. I am perplexed how people can cry and no one can ever tell. Everyone can know when I have a hard bout of crying, because my eyes swell for at least twenty-four hours. I hated going to work and have people look at me and feel sorry for me. I had the most incredible coworkers. They were so supportive. But, sometimes I wanted some normalcy. One night I just cried and cried. I was so sad and overwhelmed. I remember thinking how I was upset that everyone at work was going to know I had a bad night. I remember thinking that I should ask God to shrink the swelling before I went to work, but decided not to because it was such a small thing compared to everything else I asked of Him. Miraculously, the next morning there was absolutely no eye swelling. That may not seem important, but to me it was everything, because I knew that He cared about what mattered to me. He wanted to bless me. Again, I am welling up as I write this, because of the goodness of God.

There was a young lady with whom I worked, who was very artistic. She was a teenager. She drew a beautiful, intricate crayon drawing and brought it to me. I hung it in my office for everyone to enjoy. It was many colors put together in a way that was pretty.

Well, fast forward a few years. Shortly after Wayne's brain surgery, he had a hard time expressing himself. He could understand language and read. He could also speak words; they just didn't make sense. It would be a fifteen minute guessing game to find out what he was requesting. One day he asked for "milk with a fly in it." Huh? I tried and tried to understand. We were both getting frustrated. Finally, I went and opened the refrigerator and pointed to everything. My finger landed on the eggnog. He nodded. It is milk based and has specks of nutmeg, which represented the fly, I suppose. I left the room and melted into a heap of tears. My mom was with me and we just cried and cried together. It was such a sad time. I realized that I had lost my husband before I actually lost my husband. (He didn't completely change, but his personality and his functioning was never the same. I grieved a lot before I actually lost him, because I lost him progressively).

Within a few weeks, Wayne was able to speak effectively, but at the time I had no idea if Wayne would ever be able to communicate with me again. I was so sad. I had to work and leave him in the care of someone else. At work, I had a dear Christian friend who sat with me and prayed for me. When she was done praying, I looked up and the picture from the teenage girl caught my eye. I felt shocked. I saw a word in the picture that I had never seen before. I asked Christina if she saw the word. She did. We grabbed another Christian friend. She saw it too and started crying (This friend, Martha, was also dying of pancreatic cancer). The word was "JOY." The girl who drew the picture had moved away and was now an adult. I still had her number so I called and left a message telling her that I had never seen the word in the picture before and I was so grateful, because it ministered to me in a really difficult time. She later called back and said she didn't recall putting a word in the picture. "What was the word?" she asked. "Joy," I said. She was surprised. The night before she was with other Christians and they were praying for Christians who were suffering, praying that they would have JOY. Amazing! God is so good. I still have the picture hanging in my new office.

Are you starting to see the connection of considering it pure joy when we face trials of many kinds? I saw it.

Time passed. My grieving was hard. I still feel it sometimes. However, there came a time that I wanted to get back into work, but not full time. I decided to volunteer a little at a local crisis pregnancy clinic. It was there that I met my friend, Karen. She introduced me to my friend, Sharon. When I needed to work again, Sharon ended up hiring me at another counseling agency. I didn't think I would go back to work because of the life insurance money and investments that I made. I figured I could live on the interest. Well, I put the money from the life insurance into three large investments, two of which went bad due to illegal activity of both investment agencies. I had to go back to work. It was another huge loss, but looking back, I realize that it was what I needed to do to complete God's will for me.

While Wayne was ill, I felt I received a message from the Lord that out of my pain would be born a ministry that would wrap around a person and meet lots of needs, not just their mental health issues. I believed it and shared it with a couple of people. I just didn't know how that would happen.

Fast forward again. Sharon hired me to work as a clinical supervisor and therapist. She is a wonderful woman of prayer and touches many lives. She prayed for me daily and I believe she still does. The agency where she and I worked no longer met our needs. God was beginning His work. She went back to work for New Life Ministries. She also supported me while we began our new ministry.

A year and a half after Wayne died; I met Lloyd, my next husband to be. He had a similar vision for a new ministry and gave it a name, SPARE Ministries and Counseling Center. We decided to marry and begin the ministry. It was my ministry of pain that God gave me. Lloyd went on to do other things that the Lord put on his heart, but God gave me Lloyd to help get this ministry off and going. SPARE Counseling Center is a direct outcome of the pain that I suffered.

I am not a trained business person and I really don't like the administrative tasks involved in keeping a business. I really hate fundraising. The Lord brought people into the ministry that has helped to sustain us and have kept our doors open. We go through our ups and downs and sometimes I think it would just be easier to work flipping burgers for some fast food chain, but ultimately, I love what I do and the heart of our ministry.

One day, at a Becky Tirabassi seminar, I received another vision. It was of me standing on a Bible with my hands outreached, holding the hands of two other people. They, in turn, were holding two more hands each. It kept growing, exponentially, all the way up to the heavens, looking like an upside down triangle. I received the message that, as long as I stand on the truth of the Bible, I would facilitate reconciling of people to people and people to God.

SPARE Ministries and Counseling Center is made up of professional licensed and pre-licensed therapists who all love the Lord. SPARE is a non-profit ministry that offers quality therapy from a Biblical framework. We work on a deep sliding scale because we try to work with everyone that desires our services, even when there are financial challenges. SPARE also holds hands with other ministries and churches to provide supportive services. We give away counseling services to many as a part of our ministry. The Lord has faithfully sustained us, despite our meager revenues.

My suffering helps me minister to others in ways that no textbook ever could. I can encourage people with my professionalism, but more than that, I can minister to people, lots of them, out of personal knowledge. I can encourage them in the Lord, not just by showing them Scriptures and praying for them, but by letting them know what God actually did for me and that He can do the same for them. God is good.

Life continues to have its struggles. My new marriage was very difficult. We struggled and still struggle with finding ways to grow in intimacy. God has given me visions in order to prepare me and show me how to offer forgiveness and grace when we had rough spots. One of these visions prepared me for many of the struggles my husband and I faced. One day, while I was standing in my bedroom, I received a vision of my husband and me battling together inside of an enclosed valley (like a caldera) against an entire army. We were losing. Then, over the edge of the ridge, came a huge, beautiful white horse with wings. Its name was Grace. We were to get on the back of Grace and fly over the enemy while we fought. We would have an advantage that would allow us to win the battle. I was told that my husband would fall off of Grace's back several times and that I was supposed to ALWAYS fly down and offer him a ride back on Grace. Whether he did or not was up to him, but I needed to offer "Grace" every time. This vision was preparation for me. Without it, I do not know if we could have weathered some of the storms we faced.

God has also shown up for my husband in powerful ways to help him through the great difficulties of adjusting to a new and broken family. He suffered a lot of rejection. The Lord has often spoken healing and strengthening words directly to Lloyd, not unlike how the Lord spoke to Moses. God has been good to both of us and our story is not done.

My boys suffered a lot. They experienced depression, anger and rebellion. My boys were so young when they went through all the drama and trauma of losing their father. They had no real way of dealing with the grief other than internalizing and acting out their pain. We all received a lot of counseling as the path to healing is not so easy, but we are moving ahead and thriving. I am so proud of each of my boys. We can see the goodness of God.

The greatest thing in this suffering is knowing there is a powerful purpose if we hand our pain to the Lord. God has a plan and purpose for all of us. We don't know the whole story, but He does. Wayne used to thank God for the hard times. He understood God's perspective. Now I understand, too. He got it sooner than I did. God used Wayne's pain greatly. Wayne used to minister to the sick when he visited the hospital weekly just for the purposes of praying for people. He did this when he could not work, because he was himself dying. He arranged for a man named Joe to pick him up and transport him to the hospital weekly just so he could share the Lord with others. On one of these visits, my husband entered a patient's room who, coincidentally, was a friend of my father. My father happened to be visiting this friend at that moment. My dear husband asked her if he could pray for her. He did and then he left. This woman turned to my dad and asked him about this man that prays for people. My dad was able to tell her that Wayne was his son-in-law and he told her that he was dying from brain cancer. He went on to tell her that Wayne loved Jesus and wanted other people to experience His love. This woman (and my dad) was incredibly moved by my husband's selfless actions. Wayne was a giant in the eyes of many. While Wayne did experience some fear of the unknown, he always felt strength from the Lord. So many lives were touched by Wayne's character and love for others. He lived for Jesus while he was healthy and while he was dying. Knowing my husband's character and his love for Jesus was the greatest catalyst for spiritual growth in me. I believe the Lord brought him into my life for many reasons, but one of the greatest reasons was to grow me spiritually and prepare me for the Lord's purposes in greater ways.

So, considering my pain as an opportunity for joy is now something that makes sense to me. I am grateful that I can relate to almost everyone who comes into my office for help. There are so many other issues from my life that I cannot possibly put into this chapter, but God is using it all. Thank you Lord for helping me to persevere, and preparing me for anything.

Ana

*Let us exalt and triumph in our troubles and rejoice in our sufferings, knowing that **pressure** and affliction and hardship produce patient and unswerving endurance. And endurance (fortitude) develops maturity of character—that is, approved faith and tried integrity. And character [of this sort] produces [the habit of] joyful and confident hope of eternal salvation. Such hope never disappoints or deludes or shames us, for God's love has been poured out in our hearts through the Holy Spirit Who has been given to us*

Romans 5:3-4 (AMP) emphasis added

I was born and raised in New Orleans with immigrant parents from Honduras. In our traditional home my dad was hardworking, but a functioning alcoholic and my mom stayed home to care for her children. We lived in a modest middle-class suburban neighborhood where most families sent their kids to parochial schools in order to get a decent education.

I was the first born of three daughters. My sister, Sandra, is a year younger and my baby sister, Norma, is about nine years younger. Sandra and I shared a bedroom and we were as opposite as two sisters could be. We argued about everything. I don't ever remember feeling close to her. Although I didn't fight with Norma, I resented her. Even though my Mom didn't work outside the home, I was obligated to take care of Norma.

My father worked nights as a longshoreman and slept during the day, so I had little interaction with him. When I was home, he spent most of his time watching TV and drinking beer. He was quite impatient and had an explosive temper. I quickly learned to keep my distance. I experienced more anger than love from him, thus fear and insecurity ruled me. In fact, he was so absent from our lives that he didn't attend any of our graduations or later, our weddings.

My mom was physically nurturing in that she cooked very well and drove us and our friends to various activities and commitments. But emotional support was a different matter. She was quite reserved and not so approachable to talk to as I matured into a teenager.

Mom was religious and made sure we practiced our Catholic faith. Dad did not participate.

The only subject my parents fought about was money. They were thrifty and lived beneath their means, made regular deposits into savings and didn't use credit—all good lessons they taught me.

Because I developed quickly, from eighth grade onward I got too much attention from boys. I soaked it up since I didn't get any from my dad. This led to heavy necking, petting and sex education quizzes with friends. I now know that I gave my body away hoping to get the love and validation I so desperately wanted and needed. When I was a senior in high school, I became involved with a man who was twice my age. Somehow I got away with that under the watch of my strict parents and had sex with him once. I was so disappointed because it wasn't the wonderful experience of love that I had expected. When I let him know that, he dumped me.

After high school, I turned my back on God and church, which led to over a decade of a partying and carnal lifestyle. In my senior year of college, I fell hard for a man who used me and ended up pregnant. Scared to tell my parents, I felt forced to have an abortion. Although the procedure was quick and painless, I cried, because inside me, even at seven or eight weeks, a baby was being killed. It also turned out that the guy was crazy and using an assumed name. The Michigan police wanted him! What a painful lesson in why not to find a boyfriend in a nightclub. He went ballistic when I had the abortion and started calling my house in an attempt to "rat me out" to my parents. He even wrote "Killer Whore" on the front door of our house! Sadly, my parents knew he was crazy so they didn't believe him. This traumatic ordeal led to a season of acting out promiscuously because I believed I was a "killer whore." It didn't seem to matter, because I had lost my virginity before marriage.

Unknowingly, I was further degrading myself and my value. I felt tremendous guilt and repeatedly confessed my sins to Catholic priests. Through my twenties I had several boyfriends and always made sure of lining up a new one to replace the old one as I had no identity apart from being with a man. I wanted to get married and have a family but feared making a bad choice and ending up in a dysfunctional marriage just like that of my parents.

I was such a mess and attracted likewise: unhealthy guys and unhealthy relationships.

Because the spirits of anger and fear ruled my home, I moved out as soon as I could. As a young adult woman, I was controlling, driven by performance, did not trust my own judgment and had no boundaries. Quite a dangerous combination for a woman desiring a husband and a family!

In my late twenties, I lived with and got engaged to a man named Peter. I kept my living arrangement secret from my parents. Peter said that his mother wanted four children, she had ten and he was number six. That alone raised a warning flag. The possibility of a future together was further clouded by the fact that Peter had to take lithium for manic depression and other members of his family suffered from mental illness. All the doubts made me question whether Peter was the right man for me. My reason for getting married seemed more about turning thirty and fear that my biological clock was ticking. Indeed, my decision to marry was motivated by fear. I had returned to my Catholic faith, planned my wedding and prayed for confirmation if I should go ahead with my plans to marry Peter.

That summer I spent some time with relatives in Los Angeles and was introduced to Mike. Mike's wife had recently left him for another man and they had three young children. We had a strong physical attraction and slept together right away. As an engaged woman, I felt guilty, yet I also knew this was, indeed, the confirmation for which I had prayed. As my wise mother counseled me, we did not know if Mike was the one for me, but Peter was certainly not. Breaking it off with Peter was difficult and painful, but my decision was again confirmed when he slapped me across the face, because he figured out I cheated on him.

Mike and I had a long distance romance and he proposed to me before his divorce was even final. He might have felt like he had a gun to his head as I wasn't moving to California without his marrying me, but he didn't want to lose his rebound girl. In 1991, even though we had failed the premarital counseling tests, I moved to California to marry Mike. Our time began with a very stressful transition and we ended up in counseling right away. Looking back, the foundation for our relationship was physical, which was like building our house on sand, even though we did practice our Catholic faith as a couple. Our first Christmas together after coming home from a holiday party, he blindsided me with his declaration that he didn't love me anymore. "Devastated" fails to describe how defeated I felt. I left the house and spent the night alone in a hotel. As I was planning my escape from Mike God thwarted my plans with the news I was pregnant.

In 1992, my daughter, Meghan, was born. God used motherhood to woo me to Him and I became a Christian by accepting Jesus Christ as my personal Savior. Shortly after I became a Christian I participated in a Bible study that centered on post-abortion healing. It was there I finally experienced God's forgiveness and peace.

In 1996, about the same time I lost my job as a loan officer, I found out I was pregnant again. I had a second daughter, Lauren. The timing was right to become a stay at home wife and mom.

Unfortunately, Mike did not join me in my newfound faith and as I grew close to God, Mike pulled further away.

My embracing God and our serious financial pressures led him to file for divorce in early 2003. Once again I was blindsided by this news and did not eat or sleep for three days and ended up in a hospital emergency room suffering from vertigo. Disbelief, shock, shame and loneliness flooded my emotions. I had no local support system. I cried out to God as He finally had my full attention. I asked Him to show me my part in the marriage breakdown and He certainly did. I wrote Mike a long letter, seeking forgiveness and admitting how I had failed him as his wife.

Because we lived in Yorba Linda, California, I contacted the counseling office at Yorba Linda Friends Church. Nancy, the counseling administrator, immediately offered her help. That was the first step in my recovery journey as she introduced me to twelve step work. Through the program, I discovered that I was a codependent and an adult child of an alcoholic.

My relationship with Mike was my drug. He needed me and I needed him to need me. Our relationship was a control tug-of-war.

Around the same time, my father became terminally ill and passed away. Thankfully, I spent quite a bit of time with my Dad during his illness and had the privilege of leading him to the Lord. I finally experienced my Heavenly Father's love and acceptance for me through my earthly father's loving eyes, which I had desperately craved all of my life.

The only two men in my life had simultaneously left me. Nancy walked alongside me and met with me weekly and helped me get in touch with my feelings of abandonment and low self-worth. She was an angel sent from God who served as a tangible expression of His love for me.

Due to the painfully slow and expensive legal system, Mike and I spent the next three long years living in the same house, which was filled with great tension and anxiety. I did not have any other options financially. Mike had been counseled to not leave the house. So, we lived in separate bedrooms and tried to pretend to be a normal family. Fortunately, we kept most of our arguments away from the children. I felt imprisoned and fantasized about running away, to the point of contacting the Sheepfold Ministry for abused women and kids. I was afraid to be alone with him as I suffered emotional and verbal name-calling abuse. It was an insane, out of control situation, which didn't work for this recovering control freak. I learned that the only thing I had control over was my attitude and how I responded to the situation. God was teaching me to move from reacting to responding to situations. During those three long years, I continued to pray for Mike's salvation and for God to save our marriage. I fully expected God to intervene since the divorce was taking so long and a miserable marriage seemed like a safer option than life as a single mom.

For eight years, I had not worked. The fear of being unable to afford living in expensive Yorba Linda eventually stirred a deeper spiritual awareness. Our God is not about safety, but about stretching me to rely on Him alone for my security, not my bank balance or support payments.

I knew I needed to find work and unfortunately had few workplace skills that an employer might value. In California real estate, 2004 was a hot seller's market and I had a real estate license. I decided to become a full time realtor. That decision was also motivated by fear as I felt it was my only option to earn enough to support myself and my girls.

Our stressful living arrangement ended after a senseless heated argument. Mike filed domestic violence allegations against me. This was due to the sexual tension that existed between us. Legally married and living together, yet emotionally divorced and sleeping in separate rooms, it became clear to me that we brought out the worst in each other. That led to an extremely stressful trial where Child

Protective Services privately interviewed my girls. My oldest daughter, Meghan, was unexpectedly pulled out of school for an interview in the judge's private chambers.

By God's grace, the judge determined that Mike had exaggerated and fabricated stories in an attempt to get me evicted from the house. The judge also determined that given the level of animosity and tension, it was not safe for the two of us to continue to live under the same roof. He ordered that the girls remain in the house and for Mike and I to rotate in and out of the house, a week at a time. Because I had no income or support, I could not rent a place. Mike was able to stay at his brother's house during his out-of-the-house weeks.

Through my church body, three different families hosted me over a period of six months. This was a tough, lonely time for me as I was living out of a suitcase and very much missing my girls when it was my turn to leave. My entire identity was wrapped up in being a wife, mom and stepmom. I had no idea who I was outside of those roles. By the fall of 2006 I had finally received a small property settlement, which became my earthly security. Because Mike was self-employed and I worked as a real estate agent, I responded to my sporadic income with fear and continual worry.

The real estate market had changed dramatically. Short sales and foreclosures now dominated the business. Out of fear, I started to seek stable work. I worked as a substitute school teacher and then as a telemarketer for real estate websites. The latter was quite humbling as I worked in a very unprofessional setting. After suffering and serving my time there, my boss helped me to get a secure job working for Women of Faith to promote their event. It turned out that the telemarketing job helped me to be comfortable telemarketing churches to sell tickets. My new job was an unexpected blessing because I was paid to work for God. More amazing was that later the job served as a conduit to meet my future husband. I strived to find work suited for a single mom's need to work around her girls' schedules.

Mike and I shared 50/50 custody of the girls with a week at a time visitation. Sadly, our co-parenting relationship was just as contentious as the marriage had been. He was quite resentful about paying me support. I had to chase him for it and he would deduct whatever he felt I owed him. It became so bad that I opened a case with Department of Child Support Services so he would make payments to them and them to me. It amazed me how angry he was with me when I did not run off with another man or wipe him out financially.

His anger affected my relationships with my stepchildren. It was hurtful when his son, Chris, did not invite me to his wedding. When his daughter, Michelle, was planning her wedding, Mike did his best to stop her from inviting me. Both Michelle and her mom, Debbie, were my advocates. Because I loved Michelle and my daughters were in the wedding, I really wanted to attend. So, I decided to attend the wedding and declined the invitation to attend the reception to appease Mike. The day of the wedding I was nervous and bathed my soul in prayer. That morning God had given me a personal word in Isaiah 54:17,

> But no weapon that is formed against you shall prosper and every tongue that shall rise against you in judgment you shall show to be in the wrong. This [peace, righteousness, security, triumph over opposition] is the heritage of the servants of the Lord [those in whom the ideal Servant of the Lord is reproduced]. This is the righteousness or the vindication which they obtain from Me—this is that which I impart to them as their justification—says the Lord.

I purposefully arrived early to the wedding and sat in the back, alone and inconspicuous. Much to my surprise, Mike told me to sit up front with his family and that I would walk down the aisle after the bride's mother. Imagine the look on my face when the wedding coordinator instructed Mike to escort me down the aisle! Later my daughter Meghan told me that I should have seen the look on her dad's face! What I wouldn't have given to have seen a snapshot of this scene! After the ceremony, Mike halfheartedly informed me that I could attend the reception, but I declined. I felt elated about how God had rescued me in a very uncomfortable setting.

In my search for affordable housing in Yorba Linda, this season of survival included multiple moves, as well as another two months of staying with two different friends as temporary housing. Having to lease storage and sending my girls to stay with their dad in the interim was very painful. But I was thankful once again that God provided "much more than I could ask or imagine" of needed support through my church family.

Over the years I had lost myself so I didn't know who I was outside of the roles of wife or mother. Because I had poured myself into my girls, I struggled with letting go. I believed Mike couldn't take care of them as well as their "almighty Mom" could! So many times, I longed to run home to New Orleans to start over, but because of the girls, I was stuck in Yorba Linda, where God taught me what it really meant to trust Him.

As I was forced to assess the wreckage, recount and grieve my losses, grow from them and reinvent myself, I changed direction. I spent my free time volunteering, sharpening my job skills, in counseling, support groups and Bible study. Until then, I had lived my life out of fear and in vain trying to control my environment and those around me. I learned the meaning of true surrender, to recognize the difference between what I can and cannot control, which finally led to the peace I so desperately craved.

We were created for fellowship and crave adult connections. But I was afraid to date because I had struggled to set healthy relationship boundaries and had made bad choices. I asked God for single mom friends, which He brought me through my church body. A transformation occurred from dreading my time away from my girls to looking forward to some free time!

In the second post-divorce year, I ventured too soon into the dating world and my old patterns emerged. I wanted to be a good role model for my daughters, but it was a challenge dating as a Christian single mother. My friends and I laughed about dating dynamics for women "Forty-seven going on seventeen!"

I quickly met and became engaged to a wonderful Christian man, but that relationship lasted longer than it should have. He affirmed and built me up, which was so redeeming after being painfully rejected. Yet, I never felt peace and feared I was settling. More importantly, my daughter, Meghan, did not like him. Since one of my major concerns was how a stepfather would fit into my children's' lives, I felt conflicted. Part of me wanted to wait until my children were out of the house to get married.

After I broke off that relationship, I discovered that I did not need a man to affirm and determine my value and that I did not have to do anything to earn love. I realized I had the desire to be married again, which led to my *God's Best* list. There I outlined traits that I wanted in the man God would choose for me and determined that I would rather remain single than settle for anything less.

I am thankful that my very painful divorce led to redemption; the Lord did bring me a wonderful godly man who is more than I had ever hoped possible. Like other couples in the Internet age, we met on a Christian dating site. He admitted my connection to Women of Faith had piqued his interest. My journey finally led to a place of emotional health, freedom and readiness to be a wife again. The divorce catapulted me to a crisis of coming face to face with my brokenness. It allowed me to identify the lies that I had believed and that had ruled my life. As I pressed into my pain, I received the healing balm of Christ.

Although Mike has never taken any responsibility for his part in the breakup of our family, God has given me His heart of compassion for my former husband. By His grace alone, I have been able to forgive, release and bless Mike.

In the span of five years, the Lord turned everything around. In 2011, I got married and moved to Laguna Beach. This is the first time I have been in a relationship with a man who is safe and loves me unconditionally, just like God. Carl is my best friend and we bring out the best in each other. I am so blessed in that he doesn't care if I work, cook or clean—who I am is more than enough for him. God also led me back to sell real estate by faith, not fear. As one of the consequences of the divorce, about the same time I moved to Laguna Beach, Mike was forced to short sale the family home that he had owned for twenty-five years and rent a small apartment. I am sad for him and my girls. Meghan is away in college and Lauren has lived with me full time through high school. Lauren just graduated and is preparing to attend her dream school, Tulane, in the fall. One of my concerns as a single mom was not being able to provide college support and God took care of it, because Carl permits me to use my real estate income to support my girls.

God does, indeed, make beauty out of ashes and that has become my reality. What my former husband did to harm me, God turned into good. God has given me my heart's desires, but only after walking through tremendous suffering, healing and growth. Because I had experienced a void that my earthly father could not and did not fill, I had difficulty comprehending and receiving the love of my Heavenly Father. Gratefully, this painful journey has brought me to a place where my hunger and ache for love has been met by my God and not a man.

In Romans 5 the word "pressure" means change, which is what I believe God is working in and through me as I am clay in my Potter's hands. He used pressure to refine and mold me and I am thankful for the gift of suffering. Through my suffering I have experienced a sweet intimacy with God, which has certainly given me depth and strength of character. Because of my encounters with His deep love for me, His love has poured out through me and overflowed onto others.

My new husband and I, along with fellow co-laborers, facilitate a "Divorce Recovery/Free to Love Again Workshop," where we as wounded healers minister God's love to adults—as well as their children—who are affected by divorce. Because we have walked with God through this suffering, we are grateful that our misery has become our ministry and are privileged to offer hope to others in need.

SHARON

Some dreams you want to come true. The one I had right before Thanksgiving was NOT one of those.

Paul, my husband and I were anticipating going to visit my parents the next day with our two little boys; they were four and two at the time. The mounting excitement we all felt about going to Grandma and Grandpa's house was harshly interrupted when I awoke terribly disturbed from a nightmare that seemed more like a reality than a dream. We had been in a car accident and I was the only one hurt.

I shared the dream with Paul and my resulting reticence about following through with our trip. He shared my concern from the dream—neither one of us had experienced anything like it in our seven years of marriage. Nonetheless, he still struggled with not going. It didn't seem right to him for us to call my parents and tell them we weren't coming to Thanksgiving dinner because I had a troubling dream. Not being able to come to a joint resolve, we agreed to pray together and see if our minds were swayed in a unified direction. After praying, my husband was still resolute in following through with our travel plans. I was not, but I decided to express my fears to God by putting my trust in Him and said, "I am struggling, Lord God, but I give my fears to You. You say You will be with me, with us. Please calm my fear and help me trust in You."

We lived in Loveland, Colorado at the time, where we pastored a small Evangelical Free Church. My parents lived six hours from us, through Denver and then over the mountain passes. We readied for the trip and then all piled into the car to make our trek over the mountains. It began to snow as we reached the highest mountain pass. The roads were initially wet and clear, but they soon turned to ice as we started down the other side of the mountain. Paul slowed the car down, pumping the brakes. I had turned around in my seat to make sure the boys were doing okay when I noticed that the oldest had undone his car seat belt. I quickly helped him get it back on and connected, telling him how important it was for him to keep the seat belt hooked together. As I faced the front again, Paul noted to me that we didn't have much further to go to be down the mountain pass. Looking at each other, we both sighed deeply with relief.

Without warning, everything changed in a flash! Paul took a quick glance in the rearview mirror and saw two cars barreling down on us in the passing lane. He proceeded to move into the right-hand lane to get out of the cars' way and quickly became aware that the car now directly in front of us was going exceptionally slow. We both knew that no amount of pumping the brakes was going to put us out of harm's way. We were sandwiched between a car going too fast and a car going extremely slow. Our tires hit an ice ridge and the car began to spin. Then, the inevitable happened: we rolled down the mountainside on the other side of the road, just missing the car in the passing lane and landed upside down in the gulley next to the other side of the freeway.

Everyone in the car was stunned and awake; everyone except me. I was unconscious. Our boys had been safely kept by their car seats while Paul had been thrown on top of me. His head and shoulder had some cuts, but he seemed to be okay. A man who had seen the accident stopped to provide help. By the time he came up to the car, I had regained consciousness and was moaning that my neck was hurting and that I couldn't feel anything. The man then identified himself as a paramedic who had been trained in handling neck injuries. He stressed that I should not be moved until he could call an ambulance and get help. Paul and I were both comforted by his presence, accompanied by the command of his knowledge of skill. We wouldn't realize until later, what a gift from God this man had been to us, appearing out of nowhere, to meet so specifically the very needs that we had at that moment in time. I considered this as the first of many signs and gifts that the Lord gave me specifically along the way that He was with me, upholding me in the midst of this dire situation.

When the ambulance came, the paramedics carefully took me out of the car, placed me on a gurney and rolled me into the ambulance. I was quickly rushed to the nearest emergency center with my family following behind in another car. We soon discovered that the accident happened two to three miles from the base of the mountain pass on which we were traveling. We were not as far from the nearest mountain town and from help, as it had seemed in the storm.

Once at the emergency center, the medical staff quickly assessed my situation and determined that my spinal cord was severely damaged and that I was paralyzed from the neck down. Being aware they were going to need to take me back to Denver to get the medical help that I required, they tried to determine what the best plan of action would be because of the storm. Should they fly me in a helicopter or drive me back over the mountain pass in an ambulance? While they were assessing the situation, a nurse brought my youngest son in to see me and warmed my heart by telling me how my two boys had been playing with toys and singing songs to Jesus in the waiting room. This was the second gift and sign the Lord gave me that His presence was near.

It was decided that I would travel to a hospital in Denver by an ambulance. My family travelled separately with some close family friends my husband had called. They had lovingly driven up from Denver to the emergency clinic to support us.

I don't remember much about the long trip back to Denver, but I don't think I will ever forget being rolled into the hospital emergency room on a gurney and fixing my eyes on the first person to greet me. It was our pastor and very close friend, who I had worked with for three years while Paul and I were on staff in his church in Denver. What a comfort and reassuring sign again of Jesus saying, "I am here!" to me, especially since I had been separated from my husband on this part of the trip. We were additionally surprised when we encountered about fifty members from this same church who were waiting outside the emergency room for our arrival. It seemed that word had travelled quickly and they all gathered together at the hospital to await our arrival and pray for our trip back over the mountain, for God's healing presence, as well as His leading and guiding in medical decisions that would need to be made.

Paul had also called my parents about the accident, letting them know we would not be coming for Thanksgiving dinner and why. They quickly hopped into their car and drove the same precarious trip in the car, praying all the way! When they got close to the mountain pass, they were told the road was closed and they would have to take a different route. However, when they arrived at the place where they would have to turn off, the road was miraculously re-opened and they were able to drive on over the mountain pass to join the others who had come to support us.

Our family doctor from Denver also greeted me. Our pastor-friend had called him when he learned about the accident and knew we were coming. Being aware that I was going to need an orthopedic specialist, the doctor called the best one he knew in the Denver area to come and assess my situation.

After weighing the options, the orthopedic specialist decided to put me in traction for six weeks to give some time to let the swelling in my neck area go down. After that, they would then determine their next course of action. They would either have me wear a halo brace for several months to see if the bone and neck tissue would heal itself or if I would need surgery to fuse my neck. Despite the options, they gave us no hope that I would recover from the paralysis.

Day after day I lay in the hospital bed with screws in my head, connecting me to a contraption that was held down by bricks to prevent my head from moving. Nurses came in and out to check on me and hospital volunteers would come in and feed me my liquid food through a straw. One particular day, a new volunteer came in to hold my cup and straw while I drank. I thought it strange that she seemed to know a lot about me: namely, that I had been diagnosed with multiple sclerosis after my children were born. She asked me about the diagnosis and if I had experienced any more symptoms. I told her that I had not. I had several doctors tell me that I was either in remission or was healed. She strongly warned me not to let the doctors do surgery on my neck because going through the surgery could cause me to go blind. I'm not sure where she obtained her information, but I was greatly distressed over her conversation and the vehemence by which she expressed herself. I told the nurses that I did not want her back; that I needed encouraging volunteers, not ones giving me their own opinions or discouraging information. They gladly complied with my request.

Three or so weeks went by. Then, one morning when the nurses came to sponge bathe me and wash my feet, I was surprised to have a tingling, prickly sensation in my toes. Excitement filled the room, I actually felt something! Everyone was elated and hopeful. Perhaps the prognosis was not as dire as they had indicated. Even the doctor saw this as a good sign, but still cautioned us to take one day at a time. He had seen some situations where individuals healed completely when the feeling began to come back and others where only partial healing had taken place.

The doctor scheduled a physical therapist to come in and begin exercises to work with my muscles and limbs to see if that would help stimulate and aid in the healing process. Little by little, I began to get the feeling back in my legs and lower body. There was even some feeling in my upper body. This progress encouraged us all and gave reason to the doctors to decide to wait on surgery and place me in a halo brace to give my neck area more time to heal.

The halo brace was a mobile traction that screwed into my head and rested on my shoulders by means of a harness that covered my upper body. It might seem strange to say, but it was a welcomed change after several weeks of lying flat on my back in a neck traction composed of screws in my head and bricks that hung down the backside of my bed.

My therapy increased. Every day I was taken to the physical therapy gym where they helped me stand, get steady on my feet and slowly start the process of walking again. It was a continual reminder of how God was working in my situation. I would be rolled into the gym in my wheelchair with others who were in similar conditions: some were paraplegics; others were paralyzed from the waist down. Each person was at a different place on the healing spectrum. You could see tears in one corner and hear shouts and applause in another as everyone was challenged to stretch beyond their progress of the day before. I would leave so humbled and gratefully aware that I was daily changing from one who was a paraplegic to someone who could feel and move again.

Christmas came. I had been in the hospital for a month. The first couple of weeks Paul and our children stayed with close family friends in Denver. After my condition stabilized, Paul began to resume some of his pastoral duties again, travelling back and forth from Loveland to Denver—about one and a half hour drive each way—to be with me at the hospital. Our church family rallied around us in amazing ways, praying continually for my healing, as well as supporting Paul by taking turns to be with me when he needed to be at work. One of the ladies crocheted a hanging Christmas tree that she hung up in my hospital room. Members from the congregation had tied personalized ornaments on it to communicate their love and care. Another woman who was a hairdresser came into the hospital to cut and style my long hair so that it was easier to manage with all the metal gear supporting my neck.

In addition, the District Superintendent of our church denomination came to visit me. He oversaw the pastors in the Rocky Mountain area and was available to them for counsel and support. His visit in particular warmed and comforted my heart. I can still remember him sitting next to me, speaking to me about the presence of God being with me through all the suffering I was experiencing. He read phrases from Hebrews 13:5-6, *"For God has said, 'I will never fail you, I will never abandon you.' So we can say with confidence, "The Lord is my helper, so I will have no fear."*(NLT) These verses became a mainstay to me throughout the rest of the healing process. I would repeatedly go over them in my mind in the hospital room and be comforted as to how God had never left me. Instead He met me so tangibly; He was watching over me at the scene of the accident and never left me. Surely, I could continue to give Him my fears and trust Him to help us!

The happy day arrived when the doctor walked into my hospital room and said he could release me to go home! His medical prescription for my healing process was threefold: wear the halo brace for several months, be scheduled to come weekly to the hospital to have the halo tightened and continue with the physical therapy.

I have to admit that I met this great news with mixed emotions. Even though I had made significant progress and was eager to go home and be with my family, the reality of all that I still could not do was daunting to me! So was the fear. I questioned, "Will I ever be able to function as a whole person again?" Nonetheless, I asked myself, "Hasn't God been with me this far and not let go of me?" Recounting the tangible ways I had seen Him meet me, I reassured myself: "I can trust Him to continue to walk with me in this next part of the journey as well."

Our new regime soon fell into place. Paul's father had purchased a recliner chair that became my new resting place during the day and at night since I couldn't sleep in a regular bed with the halo brace. My mother came to stay with us for a few weeks to help us adjust to our new life. Our church family came alongside as well; coming to visit and pray for me, bringing in meals and providing daily childcare for our boys since Paul had to work and I couldn't care for them.

My whole world had changed drastically. Although I hadn't seemed to reflect on it much in the hospital, I certainly thought about it then. My life had come to a screeching halt! I had gone from being a very active pastor's wife to now doing nothing! I switched from being independent and self-sufficient to being very dependent on others to do things for me that I was used to doing myself. I had been an avid reader and now couldn't even hold a book and read to myself; others had to read to me. And being a very affectionate person of touch, one of the most difficult things I experienced was not being able to hold and hug my husband, my children or reach out to squeeze the hand of a close friend.

My external world was no longer the same, but that was not all that was different. So was my outlook! My identity had been wrapped up in the busyness of doing activities or things, whether it was for my family, friends or ministry. Now, the "doing" had been taken away and I had come face to face with the importance of "being." Life had almost been snatched from me. Now I had the chance to live and reset my priorities to that which really mattered: my relationship with God and those He had given me to love.

In some ways the next three and a half months seemed to go by quickly. This was partly because weekly we drove the long trip to the Denver hospital and back to have the doctor tighten the screws in my head that held the halo brace. I never got used to that procedure. It just seemed that I would finally get to a place where the halo brace was almost comfortable and then we'd go in to have the screws tightened and the discomfort and headaches would start all over again. Nonetheless, the time arrived where the doctor loosened the halo brace screws instead of tightening them to see if my neck could support itself without the halo apparatus. Discovering that my neck could not hold itself on its own, they were forced to screw the halo brace back on for another couple of weeks and ordered surgery to fuse my neck bone to provide permanent stabilization.

Several pastors and their wives from the community we lived in came to our house to pray for me, both for the surgery and God's healing touch. My arms and hands were the only part of my body where I didn't have full movement or feeling. Of course, I thought it would be wonderful if God would choose to heal me that night so I wouldn't have to have the surgery at all. That option turned out not to be His plan and I went in as scheduled the next week for surgery.

Not knowing what to expect from the results of the surgery, I'll never forget waking up in my hospital room after the surgery was over. I raised my arms—looking into the face of the doctor and all those standing around my bed—and asked, "How are my arms?" The doctor looked at me and said, "Well, you tell me! You're the one raising them!" We were all stunned and amazed! The fact that I could raise them at all not only shocked me but also everyone else standing there. "So what happened?!" I eagerly asked the doctor. "What did you do in the surgery that released my arms and hands?" He insisted there was nothing that they did that would have resulted in the release of movement and feeling I was experiencing in my arms and hands. We were all elated and knew that I was indeed experiencing a miracle! God had answered our prayers in a way that truly gave Him glory!

Since the neck operation was successful, I was given a neck collar to wear for three more months to enable the bones to fuse into one. Now, all that was required was to continue with physical therapy to regain the dexterity and strength I needed to have full usage of my fingers, hands and arms.

The significance of this round of physical therapy was pivotal not only to bring healing and feeling to the remaining areas of my body, but also in giving me a principle to apply to the rest of my healing emotionally and spiritually. I could raise my arms, but I was not able to stretch them all the way out. I can still hear my conversation with the physical therapist just as clearly as if it were yesterday.

"Stretch out your arms," the physical therapist said to me kindly, yet firmly.

"I can't!" I replied. "They won't budge beyond where they are!"

He then repeated his request. "I understand, but try anyway to stretch them out."

"Really!" I said. "They won't move! Am I supposed to will it to happen?" I really wasn't being sarcastic. I just couldn't understand how I was supposed to move my arms when they were locked into a position that I couldn't change.

"No. It isn't that you will it," he said. "Your arms can't move because of the pain they feel."

"What pain?" I asked. "I don't feel anything. They just won't move."

"That's because the pain is so severe, your body has shut it down," he said. "I will give you some exercises to do. As you continue to try to move your arms, you will begin to feel the pain. Then, you will know that you are making progress. Stay with it and keep trying to stretch them out."

I was stunned. I couldn't believe that there was actually feeling beyond this numbness. But I trusted what the physical therapist said and kept trying to do the exercises he gave me. I'm not sure how many days it took. All I know is that one day I sensed both feeling and pain and I knew I was making progress.

I regained all of the feeling and use of my arms and hands. I applied the same principle to my fingers when I tried to play the piano again. I can remember looking at the keys on the piano one day thinking, "How hard could it be to play the piano again? I wonder if I can just start playing one key at a time and, before I know it, the ability will come back to me?" I went over to the piano, sat down and placed my fingers on the keys. When I pressed down on the first key, I couldn't believe how heavy it felt to push down. The pain I felt pressing the key down was so excruciating that tears streamed down my face. But trusting the principles that I had applied in the other physical therapy exercises might work in this area as well; I kept at it every day. The discipline and painful effort did pay off. Eventually, not only could I play the piano again, but I also was able to type on the typewriter just as fast as I had before the car accident.

Several months passed after my neck surgery. The doctor removed the neck collar I had been wearing and I was released from all physical therapy appointments. I had a new appreciation for the lease on living life I had been given; I found myself walking every day, taking in the fresh air as if I were breathing it for the very first time. I thanked God for every step I could take, every movement of my arms I would make, including the feeling of wiggling my toes or fingers! I no longer took the movement of my body for granted! What a gift I had been given back!

But all was not well. It was not long after my last doctor's appointment that I found myself driven to constantly keep a cup of coffee in my hands, drinking the coffee throughout the day. I would go through five or more pots of coffee a day. Paul would question why I was drinking so much coffee and I would reply, "I don't question you eating ice cream, so don't question me on my coffee." But the same question nagged at me. I knew I was drinking too much coffee. The acid literally burned a hole in my stomach such that I developed an ulcer. Here I was slowly killing myself after God had reached down and healed me. What was wrong with me? I had tried to stop! I even went cold turkey only to find myself experiencing severe headaches that soon had me reaching out for another cup. Cutting down on how many cups I drank or limiting the number of pots of coffee I'd make wasn't working either. Before I knew it, I'd be right back up to the same amount I was drinking on a daily basis. One night I cried out to the Lord and begged Him for help. I told Him that

I knew I did not deserve His intervention again since it seemed I was deliberately despising the miracle He had already given me. But I knew I couldn't stop on my own.

I awoke in the morning with a strong thought, "I should alternate every cup of coffee I drank with a cup of hot water with lemon juice." I quickly challenged the thought. "Well, that certainly isn't going to work! I don't like water! Did I really think putting lemon juice in it was going to help?" Then it dawned on me that if I was questioning the thought so strongly, it couldn't be my own. Perhaps it was God helping me. I decided to give it a try. What would it hurt? Nothing had helped so far. Amazingly, within three days' time, I had whittled my coffee drinking down to almost none, drinking mainly hot water with lemon juice in its place.

In the process of exchanging the coffee for hot water with lemon, I became aware that the issue wasn't that I needed the coffee to drink as much as it was having a warm cup in my hand. The warmth brought me comfort. Comfort was the driving force. And because I drank coffee regularly before the accident, it was easy for it to become my comfort crutch. This "ah-ha" propelled me back to God. God humbled me through my recognition that I was despising His gift of healing by my inability to stop drinking. Not wanting to continue down that path, I admitted to the Lord my great need to be comforted after the accident. The pain had been so severe and intense. Going for a cup of coffee distracted me from the pain. It seemed to numb the intensity and soothe my frazzled nerves.

Needing comfort was not the only self-realization I had. I was keenly aware that I was also being tormented by the fear that the accident or "something" just as painful could happen to me again. I would push the fears down by grabbing another cup of coffee, distracting myself. I couldn't go there. I had just gotten through the physical ordeal of recovering from what had originally occurred. I certainly couldn't face the prospect of it happening again.

I had felt that God had let me down. Sure, I could recount how I felt He had reached down and seemingly met us along the way. I called it my "velvet-covered brick!" He brought someone just at the right time to the scene of the accident who knew what to do with neck injuries, brought all the people—just the right doctors, family, friends and church people, to name a few—to come alongside of us to help us and pray for us while we traversed the recovery process and certainly not least of all, had brought healing and restoration to my paralyzed body. But, nonetheless, He allowed us (me) to have to go through this agony; this painful journey. He could have stopped it in the first place by having Paul agree with me that we not go. Because that had not happened, I found myself unable to trust unequivocally, like I had before the accident, that He would keep me from ongoing harm or pain.

This tormenting fear was just as paralyzing to me as the physical paralysis I had just come through. I was limiting the trips I would take in the car and the trips Paul would make. I struggled to drive again. My world was becoming smaller and tighter around me. I was in constant turmoil and anxiety. I knew in my head that I couldn't keep another accident from happening. And I knew spiritually all the verses about giving God my anxious thoughts and fears, letting Him guard my heart with His peace—Philippians 4:6.

I was caught between allowing God to be God and trying to play God myself. The vivid picture I had in my mind's eye was of me hanging onto the precipice of a cliff by my fingertips with a terrifying long fall down. I didn't know what would be there to catch me. And I didn't know if I had the strength to hold on or know how long I was going to be able to hold on to the edge. To let go of holding on meant, to me, that I would face my fear instead of it controlling me and let go into the unknown of "trusting God". As I processed through my struggle, I told myself "fear" had not healed me. Instead, I was finding myself even more restricted than I had ever been before. God, on the other hand, had given me freedom. And yes, there was pain in making the decision we did, but God did not leave me to flounder alone through the ordeal we had been through. Instead, He met me and upheld me all along through the difficult and painful journey. There was nothing to indicate He wouldn't be there for me again.

It was during the time of this struggle that my eyes fell upon a passage in Isaiah:

> I, yes, I am the one who comforts you
> So, why are you afraid of mere humans,
> Who wither like the grass and disappear?
> Yet you have forgotten the Lord, your Creator,
> The one who stretched out the sky like a canopy
> And laid the foundations of the earth.
> Will you remain in constant dread of human oppressors?
> Will you continue to fear the anger of your enemies?
> Where is their fury and anger now?

It is gone!
Soon all you captives will be released!
Imprisonment, starvation and death will not be your
fate!
For I am the Lord your God
Who stirs up the sea, causing its waves to roar.
My name is the Lord of Heaven's Armies. (Isaiah 51:12-15 NLT)

I found myself admitting the fear and emotional paralysis to God, crying out for Him to help me trust Him again, saying that I could not continue to hold on to this precipice any longer.

I'm not sure when, but it wasn't long after this prayer time that I found myself in Isaiah again and read the following verse:

Don't be afraid, for I am with you.
Don't be discouraged, for I am your God.
I will strengthen you and help you.
I will hold you up with my victorious right hand.
(Isaiah 41:10 NLT)

The words penetrated my struggling soul. I felt like God was speaking straight to me and inviting me to let Him into my dilemma! I pondered over the words. Was I willing to give Him the opportunity to prove Himself to me again? After all, He had more than met me up to this point. I took a deep breath, surrendered and let go of the precipice. I grabbed onto His promise that His hand was there for me to hold onto. He was there for me. He would be there to help me and hold me up with His mighty hand.

Great release and freedom came in the days, weeks and years to come. Not only had I been able to break through physical paralysis with God's healing hand, but also through spiritual paralysis with the promise of His mighty, victorious hand being there for me. Yes! I could walk again and now my God was walking with me hand in hand.

Diana

*Now may the God of peace who brought up our Lord Jesus from
the dead, that great Shepherd of the sheep, through the blood of
the everlasting covenant, make you complete in every good work
to do His will, working in you what is well pleasing in His sight,
through Jesus Christ to whom be glory forever and ever. Amen.*
Hebrews 13:20 (NAS)

In my fifty-five years of living life, I have experienced several
kinds of suffering. When I cried out to God, "Why me, Lord?" I heard
Him say, in my mind, "Why not you, Diana?" That was when I
realized all the sufferings in my past were building blocks to
strengthen me and to give me a hope for the future .

I understood then that it wasn't about me at all. It was about
giving God the glory of getting me through those experiences. It was
about how I would continue to learn to give over my struggles to the
only One who could handle them, the Almighty God. He would
become my father, my mother, my friend, my comforter and my
healer.

Looking back, my first lesson in life came from being put up for
adoption. My biological family consisted of five brothers and five
sisters, including me. During the four and a half years I lived with
them, I experienced verbal abuse and physical neglect. Although the
official child welfare system tried to assist my parents, they did not
change their behavior. In the end, the three youngest of us were taken
away and put up for adoption.

My brother, who was two years older than me, went to a couple that lived in the same city we lived in and he would always run back home. My youngest sister, then a baby, was adopted into a wonderful loving family. I was a cute, tiny little blonde girl who learned to protect herself by being quiet and never rocking the boat. I was adopted into a family who had previously adopted a baby girl named Vicki, who was then seven years old,. They were loving parents and gave me the calm, steady, dependable lifestyle that I needed to feel safe and secure.

While growing up, we didn't discuss our adoptions. I later realized it was a difficult topic for my mother.

My sister, Vicki, moved out of our home at sixteen. She was in love and our parents didn't agree with her choices.

When I turned nineteen my dad was diagnosed with stomach cancer and only lived three months. I remember sitting on the back patio and journaling, "Why God? Why my dad? Why now? Now what do I do?"

I had a group of girlfriends and a boyfriend, worked and went to college. I continued my early pattern of stuffing my feelings and continued taking care of my mom and just living life.

After being married to my high school sweetheart, Rick, for two years, the miscarriages started. I emotionally handled the first one because the doctor told me that it was kind of normal and not to worry. When the second and then the third one happened, I was devastated.

Then I experienced a stillbirth at six months. This wasn't a normal delivery. My baby was stuck. It was not time for her to come down; she wasn't ready to be born. They let me push for 24 hours, with her umbilical cord hanging out, until I spiked a fever and they had to perform surgery on me. It was a horrible experience. We had already loved this baby. We had named her Jessica and had the nursery all ready for her. A part of me died the day she died.

I had learned earlier how to stuff my pain and pretend that it really didn't hurt (even though it did). I reasoned that this was another part of life. Since I already had experienced loss, I just added Jessica to my list.

But, with this loss my personality changed. I began wondering what was wrong with me. Why can't I be a mother? I was hurting inside so much and no one understood. People told me things like "It's okay, you can try again," or "Your baby is in heaven." My friends all had their babies. I would be happy for them but sad for myself, feeling the emptiness and the unfulfilled desire to have a family. They could not understand and I pretty much closed the door on sharing my pain. I didn't even know how to share it. How do you put into words the feeling that you would rather change places with your baby than go on living empty and alone? Over and over I asked, "Why, God?"

At this time we didn't have a church family and I didn't have the support I needed to get through such a loss. Rick and I grew apart. I had an affair.

In the midst of all this turmoil Rick and I recognized that we were both hurting. We recommitted ourselves to each other and to God.

We wanted a fresh start, so we sold our home and moved. Within a year we had Christian neighbors and joined their church. All was well and I became pregnant. We had the church praying for us and I thought this time would be different. We had God on our side. Again I had a stillbirth at six months. When I went on my knees before the Lord I felt like He was saying, "Will you still love me even if you don't get what you want?"

I believed in God and knew He had a plan. I felt that God had closed the door to me having any children and I was tired of trying and failing. I told Rick I couldn't try anymore; I was worn out and had no energy left to try.

The next morning a Catholic nun came around and asked if she could talk with me. I shared my situation with her, telling her how I was giving up and felt I couldn't do it anymore. She prayed with me and I felt warm from the top of my head down to my toes. I felt such peace and the desire to try again to have a baby came upon me.

When Rick came in later that day I shared with him what had happened and how I wanted to try again. He was in shock, but so happy at the same time.

ಬೊಂಞ

God knew how much I wanted a family and He allowed it to happen, but not without a lot of twists and turns. Not only did God give me my own children, He also allowed me to reconnect with my birth family. It happened in this way. I wrote a letter to my home state of Ohio to find out any information on my birth mother, using my last name from my adoption paperwork. Two weeks later I got a call at five a.m., telling me they matched my letter with another letter that had been sitting there for a year.

I came from a family of ten counting me. They all lived in Ohio. My youngest sister, Dorothy, had found the family first and had asked if this was all of us. They said, "No, there is one sister three years older than you that was adopted and we have never heard from her." So she wrote a letter and tried to find me. Her letter sat in an office for over a year.

Rick and I flew out to Ohio and met them all. Everyone was there but my birth father, who had died. Finding my family was a huge deal. The story was even written up in my hometown newspaper.

One thing I learned at this reunion was that during her pregnancy with me, my birth mother had taken a drug for nausea that might have contributed to all my miscarriages.

⅜⅓

With time and perseverance I was blessed with three beautiful, unique children and a husband that loves me very much. I would like to share that each one came into this world "special" and each one was a time of trusting in God and believing that He knew my heart and knew that I wanted a family.

Jonathan was born first. I spent four and a half months in the hospital, off my feet. I almost lost him a few times. It was so hard to hand him over to God and trust that God's will was for my son to be born. I struggled to hold on to the belief that God knows, that God hears us when we pray.

The elders of our church would come on Wednesday nights and pray for us and anoint Jonathan with oil. He would kick and jump in my womb when they prayed.

I had an angel of a nurse, Denise, who made things a little easier by giving me "special treatments," like washing my hair or shaving my legs. Nurses' work is hard and I appreciated each and every one of the angels in disguise who took care of me.

During those months we came up with an idea of putting a large calendar on the ceiling and marking off each day with an X to show me how far I had come and how much longer I needed to stay.

After being in the hospital from October to February and getting ready for delivery, we came to a day when our unborn baby's heart rate dropped. My doctor, who was like a brother now since I'd been seeing him every day for four and a half months, said to me, "Do you trust me?"

"Of course I trust you," I replied.

"We have worked too hard to get your baby here," he said. "We are not going to lose him now. I'm taking you in for an emergency C-section."

"Okay," I agreed.

As Rick was walking in from clearing out the hospital room I had lived in for all those months, he saw the doctor running down the hallway, with me on a gurney. Hospital staff opened the surgery room doors and instantly began putting in I.V.'s and throwing iodine on my stomach. The next thing I knew I was out.

Rick walked into the operating room just as they were pulling a crying Jonathan out.

With our second child, Amanda, I stayed at home in bed and had a monitor to keep the doctor informed of my contractions and medications to control those contractions. I delivered her at six pounds, five and a half ounces by C-section and was awake for the whole birth.

Lacie was our last child. We fostered her first and then adopted her at five and a half.

It was a challenge working with the county. The adoption process seemed to take forever. Although Rick and I had dreamed of adopting, the process made me relive my memories of being adopted as a four and a half year old. It triggered my feelings of abandonment and I had a lot of anxiety. I became depressed and had a hard time handling life with three small children. Our business was busy and Rick wanted to be there, but he was torn between keeping the business afloat and caring for me. "Which fire do I put out first?" he would say.

At that time we thought it best that Lacie live with a half-sister. I went into counseling for a year and worked through all those abandonment issues. I came to understand that Jesus had been with me, even in my difficult days, loving me and protecting me.

Through the social worker, Lacie had sent Amanda a birthday card and so we called to see how she was doing. At that time she was being moved for her best interest and they were looking for a place for her to live. We went into deep prayer asking God for a miracle to bring Lacie back to us to live with us.

God made it happen. Lacie came back to be with us and finally became ours forever. I'll never forget how God worked this all out.

Being blessed with all three children really helped me mature in the Lord. Seeing how He gave me the desire of my heart helped me trust Him and to believe His word, qualities I would need in the next season of my life.

&0C3

In 1999, a lump on the outside of my right breast turned out to have another name: *ductal carcinoma in situ*. Breast cancer. I was forty-one and my children were eleven, nine and seven.

I felt overwhelming fear. This was first time I had been close to death. All I could think about were my children. Who would take care of them?

The decisions that needed to be made were unbelievable. Did I want to save my breast and do a lumpectomy or have a bilateral and remove both breasts? Did I want to shave my head or let my hair fall out on its own? I had never thought of losing either my breasts or my hair and now I had to make a decision on both! I loved my breasts and I loved my hair. I couldn't cut them off.

I remember talking with Rick and realizing that it was too much to lose a part of me. I couldn't do it. I chose to do the lumpectomy. They removed the breast cancer, a little normal breast tissue around the lump and some lymph nodes under the arm. When they received the pathology report it showed they had not gotten clear margins. The following week I had to go back under and have more tissue removed to get clear margins.

I went through the five chemo treatments. I found it easier mentally to do the treatments for the sake of someone else rather than just for myself, so I dedicated one to each child, one to my mom and one to Rick. I decided to shave my head so that I could be in control of my hair loss. My mother-in-law, Hazel, bought me my first wig.

Since radiation decreases the risk of cancer coming back in the remaining breast tissue, I had twenty-seven radiation treatments, all in Los Angeles. I would take a bus from Riverside and back to Kaiser. We would all get on the bus and wait until we each had done our treatments and then return home. It took us all day.

After all the treatments, I was given a pill, Tamoxifen, to take every day for five years. It helps prevent your body's natural hormones from reaching the cancer. It is like a lifeline you take, hoping that the cancer doesn't return. It has side effects, which I struggled with: horrible bone pain in my legs, hot flashes, headache and weight gain. I decided to stop taking the pill in year three.

I was asking God why I was experiencing what I was `and was open to what He was trying to show me. Part of what I heard was that allowing others to help me during my time of illness not only aided me but also gave joy to my helpers. It was a hard lesson for me to learn because I'd rather give than receive.

Nine years later I had to take a refresher course in the lessons I had learned. The cancer came back on the left side. This was a different cancer which grew down the milk ducts into the breasts and spread into one lymph node under my arm. Again, emotions flooded me and I asked "Why Lord? I did it once, isn't that enough? What have I not learned? What are you trying to show me?"

My challenge this time was to figure out if I should remove the right breast, which has already been taken care of with the surgery/chemo/radiation, or let it stay and remove only the left breast. I couldn't trust that my right breast was already taken care of. I kept thinking that the cancer could return there also.

While waiting for the surgery, I went through the chemo first to shrink the tumors in the left breast. I ended up getting sick, which turned into dehydration and spiked a fever. I spent time in the hospital fighting a major infection. While I was there, the doctor gave me meds that I apparently was allergic to and didn't know it at the time. I was not able to sleep and was restless. I kept having weird dreams of dark places and it scared me. I prayed, "Lord, help me." Feeling desperate, I said, "If you're really here with me, Jesus, give me a sign. I need help."

As I fell back asleep it was like I was seeing the dark, deep water at the bottom of the ocean. Exhausted, I cried out to Jesus to help me. The sand turned light brown and in the sand I could make out faces of my loved ones who had died: my dad, mom, father-in-law and Jesus' face. It brought me such peace. I knew I was going to be okay.

The next day I told my doctor I was seeing things. He then told me I might be allergic to the medicine. For me, I know the miracle was given to me to give me strength.

After the chemo was completed, surgery was scheduled. I had to go see a surgeon and Rick came with me. When we got to the room I got undressed and put on the white gown. Rick sat across from me in a chair and I was up on the flat table. I had tied the gown in the front and made sure I was completely covered. The doctor came in. He sat down so that the three of us formed a triangle. He introduced himself seriously and started to explain the procedure. I sat there, watching the doctor and occasionally glanced at my husband. All of a sudden I saw Rick trying hard not to laugh, with his hand over his mouth. I gave him a puzzled look and Rick pointed at me. The doctor was still talking and with a solemn face, looking straight at me. I glanced down and saw that my gown had fallen open, showing my entire right breast. I looked at Rick and he was almost falling out of his chair with laughter. I started laughing too, but the doctor just sat there as if nothing was wrong. We pulled it together and finished listening to the doctor. As he left, we started laughing so hard Rick couldn't get his breath.

Even throughout the tough times we found ways to laugh. It helped with the stress.

In spite of the doctor's recommendation, I decided to remove both breasts. Rick and I talked it over and he assured me that he supported me with whatever I decided to do. He told me that he would love me the same no matter if I had breasts or not.

We prepared for when I would come home from surgery. We moved the recliner into our bedroom and figured out Rick would be the one to help me get in and out of the chair. When you remove your breasts you are not allowed to use your arms for pulling or pushing for several days. You have drains that need to be emptied and fluid that needs to be tracked. That is the last place you want to look.

I had no idea how devastating it would be to lose a part of my body. I could not have reconstruction at the time of surgery because they had to get clear margins, which they did not. A week later they had to go back in and remove more tissue, which they took down to the bone. I was in shock and couldn't believe I was doing it all over again. I was running in that same race I thought I had finished.

I trusted the Lord and knew there was a purpose. I felt that this time my suffering was for someone else and that I was the vessel that God was using for His Glory. Looking back, I see how there was more that I needed to learn. This was for me again.

I had been struggling with wanting to be accepted and loved for what was inside my heart, not my physical appearance, even though Rick continually showed me that he loved me and that we were soul mates. He wasn't going anywhere.

I am not a vain person, but with this second cancer bout I really struggled with wanting to feel "normal." I had no hair and now no breasts. Everywhere I looked I saw breasts. I didn't feel like I was sexy, or for that matter feel like a woman. I had tried the prosthesis that you put in your bra, but they were too heavy and the bra was too tight. I couldn't find clothes to wear. Every top they sold seemed to be low-cut. I was always afraid my scars were showing. Wearing no prosthesis made me look too flat and I felt I was being stared at for being different.

I remember I came home one evening and pulled my prosthesis out of my bra and laid them on the side arm of the couch while I was watching TV. My daughter, Amanda, came in and sat on the couch across from me. I got up to get something and one of my prosthetic breasts fell to the floor. I looked at her and she looked at me. "It's a good thing your brother is not here," I said. "I would have scarred him for life. It's not every day you see a breast on the floor." We laughed and hugged each other.

My struggle with God about feeling normal was a daily occurrence. I couldn't let it rest. I was unhappy and kept searching for an easy fix but I wasn't getting any answers. My appearance was unacceptable to me.

At the time Rick was working a lot of hours trying to keep the shop going and wearing a lot of different hats. He supported me in whatever I felt I needed and encouraged me to get whatever would help me feel normal. I shopped online and found some stick-on breasts, which I immediately bought with my credit card. This was the answer for me; I would be a new woman. Sadly, this did not fix my problem. They were not trustworthy; they would just drop at any time and any place, which caused me many embarrassing moments.

This part of my life consumed me and I felt so inadequate. Your mind can play tricks on you and you start believing the lies that the commercials sell you. God's answer is found in 2 Corinthians 10:5 where we are told to, "use our powerful God-tools for smashing warped philosophies, tearing down barriers erected against the truth of God, fitting every loose thought and emotion and impulse into the structure of life shaped by Christ" (The Message). Gradually, I began to realize that I am a princess of the most High God. He loved me and formed me in my mother's womb. I needed to continue to believe the words of my God and not the worldly view that breasts and long silky hair are what makes a woman.

I was talking with a friend who had a friend going through cancer and she asked if I would share my past experiences with her. I said I would love to. We shared with one another and I added her to my prayer list. I have to say I was thinking in the back of my mind, "Lord I hope you're not preparing me for another cancer reoccurrence.

Surely not." A couple weeks later I had a regular checkup planned. I didn't think anything of it and even went by myself. Well, guess what? My cancer numbers were up even though I was feeling fine. My back was hurting some from a heavy box I picked up from work, or so I thought.

The doctor said we had to hunt for where the cancer was in my body. The tests showed the breast cancer had gone to my bones. They call that "metastatic breast cancer."

I was now faced with cancer for the third time. They still needed to find out what kind it was, so a bone biopsy was scheduled. I was so scared. I remember thinking, "This is the worst thing ever." I requested to be knocked out completely so not to hear or see anything. To get to the hip, they had to go through my buttocks, so I had lain down on my stomach. I ended up waking up and hearing the sound of a drill and feeling sharp pain. I let out a cry for help. The anesthesiologist said "I'm here," and I was out like a light. The results showed that the cancer had metastasized from the breast cancer in 2009.

For my treatment my oncologist suggested a "port," which is surgically implanted under your skin in your chest area. It goes into the main artery of your heart. The chemotherapy drug is then put in the port along with any other drugs that may be needed. This makes infusion so much easier. Both my arms were used previously with the other two cancers and my veins would not hold up for another round of chemo. The port surgery went smoothly and I was pleased to have it behind me. The treatments were then given through the port and took more than seven hours each time to "drip" all the medications into my body. They then gave me drugs to help me handle the drugs.

This last invasion of cancer to my bones was diagnosed in June 2012. I went onto Facebook and shared with my friends how I was struggling with the news of cancer again.

I posted about how my journey was decided and how I felt I was sitting in the front seat of a roller coaster ride and hanging on to the bars, praying that I would make it through. I said, "I don't like roller coasters: the height, speed and twists all make me sick. I know all my friends are sitting in the seats behind me, some are giggling, laughing and talking . . . I hear some yelling out to me, 'Diana, you're going to be ok, hang on tight.' Some are praying to give me strength to relax and let it go. I believe that Jesus is in the seat with me and all my family and friends are behind me 100%."

Along with my Facebook friends, I had my mother-in-law who was an angel sent from God to watch over me. Things happened to me when she wasn't with me. One time she couldn't make it to my chemotherapy and I ended up yanking out my port needle while in the bathroom. I stepped on the extra length of tubing and blood shot out everywhere. I didn't know what to do first: wipe myself or pull the cord for help. I didn't want the door opening with me on the toilet but yet I didn't want to bleed to death either. I joked with my mother-in-law later, telling her all that had happened because she wasn't there. She good-naturedly promised to never leave me.

My church family supported me by bringing me soups because that was all I could manage. They each made soups and froze them and all I had to do was defrost them when I needed them. Another time they asked if I would like someone to come clean my house; I instantly said "No," thinking I didn't need someone doing the things I could do. I was still learning during this time that letting others help you not only helps you but also gives the other person joy. After reconsidering, I called Julie and told her I would love to have someone come and clean for me. Since I suffered with sores in my mouth and down my throat and back pain all the time, I took pain pills every five hours. The drugs made me so tired that I didn't have energy to do anything. The timing for housecleaning help was perfect. I walked out and found three people working so efficiently that they even cleaned my toaster and appliances that I never had time to clean. When I came back out a few hours later they were gone, so I laid down on the couch, just in awe of how beautiful they had made my kitchen. It sparkled. I felt as if each one of them had washed my feet.

Another major side effect was that the treatment affected my taste buds. I could not taste any food at all. I didn't want to believe this was how I was to live the rest of my life. I was angry with God. Then, after praying and seeking peace, I realized that God didn't have to bless us with taste. He gave us taste buds because He loves us. My perspective changed and I began sharing with others how lucky they were to still taste a good steak or eat a crisp green salad. All my vegetables and fruit had to be cooked to remove any bacteria since my resistance was lowered by the chemotherapy. I lost weight and my doctor urged me to eat anything I could.

I slept on the couch in our living room because I had better back support and I had a view of our backyard. We started feeding the birds and found out that they would come if you fed them. I had a hawk come almost twice a week. I had a squirrel eating out of the bird feeders and ducks would fly in and eat off the ground. I felt such a peace with nature right out my window that I could see from my couch.

When my numbers started going up, my drugs were changed and a new chemo was started. It killed the cancer cells and brought down the numbers. But, it also had the side effect of "hand and foot disorder." It was a painful burning heat that starts from inside your hand and works outward. Your hands and feet peel from dry skin. My face and neck were also affected and were being burned. I looked like I was spending time at the beach I was so brown. My fingernails were lifting and I would hide my hands from their ugly appearance. The chemo was doing too much damage to my body so the doctor put me on an antibiotic and reduced my medicine.

Missing a chemotherapy treatment can be a huge let down. That happened to me and I went into a panic attack. I got confused about what I was taking and the side effects and told the doctor I wanted to change what I was being given. I had to call my husband and ask him to help me remember. Once I was clear minded I told them I wanted my chemo and they had to call the doctor to get it approved. When you are on chemo, you have momentum going and it feels like a race you are trying to finish. Stopping treatment for illness adds weeks and months onto the process, which I didn't want. I always wanted my chemo.

In both 2009 and 2012, my white cells dropped after the chemo was given and I was given shots to bring them back up. The shots attack your bone marrow, causing it to multiply, which brings more white cells to fight and heal. I would get the shots five days in a row in my stomach and my husband signed up for the job. I had mixed feelings about him through those days. I loved him, I hated him. The shots gave me horrible bone pain but they helped increase the white cell count, which enabled me to get my next chemo treatment.

Since this was my third bout with this disease, I made changes in my life that brought joy and laughter. My hair was affected on the fourteenth day of my first chemo cycle so I went and bought different colored wigs. I had a red wig, a dark brown wig and a long blonde wig. Rick didn't even recognize me when we were out once. He walked right by me. I finally picked one, the red one and wore it the most. At church one Sunday the pastor's wife asked if I was there. He paused for a moment and said, "Yes, she's in the red today."

We owned our own business and one day, when I was working late and was hot, I took off my prosthetic breasts and laid them in the desk drawer. I forgot to put them back on and drove home. I was embarrassed but called up Rick and asked him if he could get in the drawer and bring me my boobs home. We laughed. Not every wife calls and asks for that kind of favor.

As my kids got older, they were able to handle all my physical changes better, so I felt free to go without my wig whenever I wanted to. This broke the ice with people and gave me opportunities for conversations that normally would not have surfaced.

As I write this I know that my count has gone up so we are changing the meds again. I also know that my bone cancer will never be completely gone. They say you can live with bone cancer for years; you are just in pain.

Knowing that I will always have this cancer reminds me of how the apostle Paul suffered with an affliction. He learned that God was enough, no matter what. My cancer reminds me of this, too.

I am also reminded of how God asks those who have faith in Jesus Christ to stand up and be different. I feel like during the days when I struggled with looking different and tried so hard to get back the normal in my life, I was growing. I was learning to see who I really am and what is really important in life. When I start to feel like I don't fit in I remember, "Jesus, You are my strength in my weakness. You carry me. You are my everything." I don't ask God "Why me?" anymore because I know why. He is in control and has a purpose. I believe He gives us today to live to the fullest.

My abandonment issues ran deep. It took me years of trusting God in small steps and seeing Jesus with me through the small and big struggles in my life before I could come to a place of healing.

When the cancer went to my bones it was like God was showing me what was important. He allowed me to go to the next level to learn more about Him. He never left me. I see now that He was with me because I called to Jesus and asked Him to be with me. He became a part of my life when I invited Him in.

Jeremiah 33:3 says, "Call to Me and I will answer you and show you great and mighty things, which you do not know" (NKJV).You too can find Him when you have eyes that see and ears that hear. Seek Him above all else. Living life and being alive in Him is more important than whether we fit in or how we look.

I am grateful to share my story with every one of you who has picked up this book. My dream has been to use my sufferings for your gain. If you can take anything from what I have shared, it is all worth it.

Amanda

Publisher's Note: Amanda was introduced on page 62. She is Diana's daughter. Here is her perspective on her mother's journey.

I don't remember my mother's first fight with cancer all that clearly, just little snippets of memory that are fuzzy around the edges. I remember when she sat us down and told us that she was sick, that something was wrong with her breasts. I was in fifth grade at the time and had never encountered any kind of serious illness. In my mind, cancer wasn't something to be afraid of, not yet.

When the cancer came back the second time, I had just gotten back from a trip to Japan. I came through the door, happy and thrilled and exhausted from the plane flight and I took one look at my mom and knew something was wrong. As I grew older, it became easier for me to read her and with one look I knew that whatever she was going to say, I wasn't going to like it. I remember her insisting on telling me later, that it could wait, but I kept badgering her until she finally confessed that her cancer had come back. I remember the terror I felt in that moment, no longer shielded by naiveté and the childish belief that my parents were godlike figures of strength. Instead, I'd looked at my mom and seen how vulnerable she was, how a few mutating cells could steal her away from me.

I remember hugging her and crying, swearing into her hair as I held her that if God took her away from me then He didn't deserve my love or respect. That I would hate Him. How could I love a God that would take my mom away from me, a woman that loved and respected God, her faith so strong that sometimes I felt like I could almost see it, a palpable force filling the air around her?

The third and last time, the cancer returned, I was receiving acceptance letters from the different colleges I had applied to. I had been toying with the idea of going to UC Santa Cruz, but with the news that my mother's cancer returned the answer was obvious: I would go to UC Irvine and stay at home. UC Irvine was a twenty minute drive away so it was the perfect solution. When I told Mom my plans, she sat me down and told me while she would love for me to stay home, she also wanted me to get the "full college experience," as she put it. She said I should go to Santa Cruz, because, after all, I would be able to come home for holidays and we would be able to call or text whenever we wanted.

With her advice, I decided to go to Santa Cruz. I came home for every holiday and even sneaked home a few times to surprise her. It wore on me to be so far away when I knew my mom was sick. I constantly questioned my decision to leave, wondering if I was being selfish. Every time I came home and then left to go back to school, my mom was a little thinner, moving a little slower as her body was worn away by pain and drugs. By the time I was ready to graduate, my mom was skin and bones and just looking at her hurt because I had left her behind when she needed me. Her pride in me as she watched me walk across the stage and receive my diploma made it worth it, to some degree.

So I came home, the triumphant daughter with her shiny new degree. The plan was for my mom to start training me in her job at my father's business and that way I would give her more time to rest and start earning money towards paying off my student loans. In the meantime, I was so happy to be home where I could finally watch over my mom and make sure she wanted for nothing. She spent most of her day on the couch by this time since the pain made it difficult for her to sleep and my dad's snoring certainly didn't help. I sat with her for hours, watching movies and just talking, or driving her to her appointments or to the store when she felt strong enough to go shopping.

About a month after I came home, I was sitting in my room playing a video game or something, and my mom walked in. She said her stomach had been bothering her for a while and she was going to go to the hospital to see if they could figure out what was going on. I asked her if she wanted me to take her, that I would be more than happy to, but she just shook her head and said she would be fine. She made it to the door before she stopped, turned around and came back to me. She leaned in to kiss me on the forehead and told me she loved me. I remember smiling, saying something sarcastic that slips my mind now and telling her I loved her too.

Later, my sister woke me up at four in the morning. She told me that Mom wasn't doing well, that she might not survive the night and we needed to get to the hospital. Later on that day, at 11:30 a.m., July 13, 2014, my Mom finally found relief from her pain in the arms of the Lord.

I had known that day was coming for months now, could see it in the slow deterioration of her body as pain and drugs chipped away at her. But even being braced for it, nothing could have prepared me for the awful reality of her death. Even now, almost a full year later, it still takes my breath away to know that she's gone. There are no words to describe the hole her death has left in my family.

What I can say, though, is that her faith never wavered nearing the end of her time. Even as the pain gnawed at her bones and the drugs dulled her mind, my mom was at peace, her belief in the grace and power of God a palpable force. She never stopped believing that her pain and illness were God's plan, her trust in Him and His plan absolute. Her faith was humbling at times and thinking back on it now, I'm still a little in awe of her. She lived in the word of God and never hesitated to share it with others. My mom believed with all her heart that her cancer was a trial with purpose and so sought out others who were also struggling with cancer and shared her faith. She touched so many lives with her caring and love for God and she told me herself that if it weren't for her own illness, she would never have been able to reach them.

She was so strong and full of life, determined to share it all even as it dwindled. Her kindness and strength live on in every life she touched and if even one soul turned to God with her guidance, I think she would find that a fitting tribute to her sacrifice.

In regards to my own faith, I struggle with it daily. I find it hard to trust a God that stole my mother away from me, especially one who loved and trusted Him the way she did. But in honor of my mother I have not fully turned away from Him. Surely a God who managed to earn my mother's love and devotion is worth knowing and maybe one day I will be able to forgive Him. I think my mom would understand.

I miss you so very much, Mom and I hope that one day we can be together again.

Jane

Before I formed you in your mother's womb, I knew and approved of you.   Jeremiah 1:5 (AMP)

My suffering has mostly been self-inflicted. I was my abuser. For years, "God save me from me" was the theme of my prayers. But God "set my feet on a rock and gave me a firm place to stand. He put a new song in my mouth,"(Psalm 40:2-3). He has transformed the invisible wall that separated me from Himself and my fellow man into the path on which I meet with Him and with my fellows.

I've had *It* as long as I can remember. I couldn't stop _____ (fill in the blank). There's always been something I could not stop doing even though *It* left me feeling empty, ashamed and alone. Sometimes there were physical consequences, but those were much easier to bear than the anguish in my heart and mind. I'd take physical pain over emotional and mental turmoil any day.

It has often looked like me losing control: being falling-down drunk when it wasn't "that kind" of a party; throwing up before the party started; horrific hangovers from drinking and binge-eating; not knowing anymore what was a "normal" portion of food; swinging helplessly from an all-consuming binge to a period of starvation; guiltily sipping my wine or liquor, fearing I might appear as eager for the affect as I actually was. *It* was a paranoid mind—not knowing what people did or didn't know about me and suspecting everyone was of ill-will, including those closest to me. It was the dynamite of emotion inside of me that would explode on the last person I would want to hurt because I couldn't hold *It* a second longer. *It* was feeling overwhelmed by things that "normal people" did every day with little thought, such as answering the phone, showing up to work, knowing what to say, making a decision, being a daughter, a sister, a friend, an aunt and a co-worker. I would analyze what people thought of me and how I could be who they expected me to be, but I usually failed miserably, at least in my mind. I couldn't stand to see my family feel pain or be disappointed; the inability to protect them and having to watch them hurt was too much for me. My inability to accept these things propelled me to escape into whatever pleasure I was using at the time to distract me from the problems of living, something to make the bad and scary feelings go away. *It* was the fact that whatever I used as a solution eventually became my problem. And then, *It* actually caused the bad, scary feelings: shame, remorse and sometimes terror. "God save me from me!" *It* began and ended with a sense of apartness from God's love and light and from other human beings.

As a little girl, I had a hard time looking at myself in the mirror. I hated my face, partly because I couldn't stand my freckles, nose and chubby cheeks, but mostly because I couldn't stand who I thought I was inside. I sensed that I was bad and feared what people thought or knew about me. This was ironic because I received a lot of love from my family and friends. The youngest of six kids, my family knew me as a roly-poly, affectionate and smiley baby-girl and then an animated, silly, little kid.

Growing up, I received affirmation and praise from my peers and adults. Attracting friends came naturally to me, which was inconvenient because I'd rather be alone. The older I got, the more uncomfortable I felt with people. I couldn't articulate it at that time, but the word was ANXIETY. I only knew that my stomach sometimes hurt and there was a constant chatter within me about what the right thing to say would be, what she felt, what he thought and how I needed to control and manage those things. I wasn't aware that I was attempting to fill God's shoes, as if I could read everyone's mind and know what "should" be. I was carrying the weight of the world on my shoulders instead of knowing that He has the whole world in His hands. I didn't know how to do what it says in Psalm 46:10, "Be still and know that I am God."

As I grew up, these feelings intensified as my peers became increasingly social and I became increasingly awkward. My outsides portrayed a completely different story than the reality of my insides. I realize now that my thoughts and feelings are only my perceptions, not "reality." But at the time I didn't know there was a difference. As a teenager, I continued to attract friends, getting a lot of invitations and struggling through those events when I didn't have an excuse not to go. But as high school went on, I felt things changing. At this point, we were becoming individuals with responsibilities and expectations and I saw my reflection in people's eyes changing from a happy go-lucky high-schooler to a lost and troubled girl, a kind of "Dr. Jekyll and Mr. Hyde." Some of my teachers would've said I was a conscientious and sweet student, but others knew me as a disrespectful student with an attitude-problem, challenging their reasonable expectations as my teachers. People remarked about my bright smile and that it seemed impossible for me to get angry, while my mom was very familiar with my explosive temper. My sister witnessed my rage at the image in the mirror on more than one occasion and my boyfriend experienced firsthand my inability to control my temper, kicking the dashboard of his car in a fury and hitting him in a fit of hurt. I was a dichotomy of the sweetness I exuded and the raging misfit that I struggled to conceal. My perception of myself depended on whose eyes I was looking into because I had no sense of self other than what the reflection of their eyes told me. I existed from the outside in. What they saw was all that mattered, because they could not know the truth, which I avoided thinking about as much as possible. I was afraid of who I was.

I don't know how much of my fear came from my own behaviors and need to conceal them and how much of it came from an over-sensitive conscience and a nervous disposition. But fear dominated me: fear of the dark, fear of entering a room full of people, fear of saying the wrong thing, fear of having to be on someone else's terms (such as staying at someone else's house and being on their schedule), fear of having a heart attack, fear of hurting people's feelings; it was endless really. Sometimes I would start thinking about my breath and get panicked that I wouldn't get enough air. I didn't want to tell anyone because I was afraid. What if something serious was wrong? I'd rather not know.

I can recall a few times throughout the years when I would hear about some individual who was well loved as being a particularly kind or joyful person, who then shocked everyone around them by committing suicide. Those left behind were perplexed by it and responded in disbelief, but I was not surprised. I felt a kindred spirit with them; they probably felt how I felt; they were hiding too. I felt I understood what they might have been going through. That scared me. Of course, I could never talk about that; "Sshhh," *It* would say.

By college I was no longer attracting friends. This was a relief but also a slap in the face. I didn't want to have to struggle through relationships, but wanted to be wanted and all of a sudden I wasn't. Who was I? I felt myself becoming "the weird girl," the kind of person I'd always felt sorry for. I spent the majority of my time alone in the dorms, perched on my bunk bed when I wasn't in class or at meals. My life consisted of talking to my boyfriend, writing letters to him and thinking about him. My boyfriend had become my drug of choice. My antisocialness progressed at a time in life when socializing was the name of the game.

In the year that King Uzziah died, I saw the Lord ...(Isaiah 6:1). The first time I heard this verse I thought, *That's what happened to me!* The year I fell out of love with Mike, I awakened to the living God. I was twenty. I woke up next to Mike one morning thinking, *If I believe in God, why am I ignoring Him?* Today I know that thought was not my own, but a gift from Him. A series of "coincidences" followed. I was invited to church by two girls my age that came into the Jamba Juice where I worked. I know now they were sent by Him. I agreed to visit their church and was amazed by a family who shared about their experience of moving across the world to share the love of God in a country where the law mandated that they be killed for doing so. They gave up everything out of their love for God and people. For the first time I began to understand that God is not "once upon a time," He's NOW and people are actually responding to Him with their lives not just acknowledging that He exists.

It was shocking to me when I fell out of love with my boyfriend. The pain was excruciating. Through other losses, I'd felt numb and puzzled when I observed people around me feeling so deeply. I chalked up the discrepancy to my "badness," oblivious to the fact that I was using whatever pleasure I could find as a "stopper" for my feelings. But with this loss, I felt the pain at my core. There was no evading it. Until then, I could not get enough of my boyfriend: he had become my world. I felt the floor had dropped out from under me.

While going through the long and agonizing process of breaking up, I met a girl outside of one of my college classes who I was strangely drawn to. I actually initiated the conversation. I wanted to know if she thought I should go into the class even though it was half over or if I should wait until it ended to turn in my paper. My boyfriend and I had been having a passionate relationship "discussion" and I'd lost track of time. Her name was Michelle. I know now that God came to me through her. After talking for the remaining fifteen or forty-five minutes of waiting, she invited me to a Bible study. I said yes. I'd been asking God to show me if He was real because I needed to know whether or not anybody was actually hearing my prayers. This was His answer.

One night I found myself on the phone with Michelle complaining about the absurd ideas some people in that Bible study had been talking about. I was angry and disgusted. They took the words of Jesus literally when He said, ""I am the way and the truth and the life. No one comes to the Father except through me". (John 14:6). "Fanatics, that's not love!" I said, as if I knew what love was.

Following a couple of traumatic days of research, prayer and conversation, I was convinced. Jesus is God. And, He is love. And, I needed forgiveness. He took care of it for me before I even knew He existed. My eyes were opened. I asked Him to take my life, do with me what He would; make me His own and cover me with His purity and His protection. I was reborn. It was like my entire life I'd been sleeping and now I was awake. As if I'd been seeing in black and white and now I was seeing in color. In the days that followed, I was actually seeing and hearing for the first time. The songs I heard on the radio talked about a quality of love only He could give. Billboards looked different—instead of the illusion that was being pedaled, I saw what was being sought and falsely promised: a sense of adequacy, satisfaction, security, freedom, power. God was the only one who could fulfill these needs and He was willing and able! People's conversations sounded different. I perceived that some were spiritually asleep and some were awake. I found myself praying for strangers I saw on the street; it was God's heart beating in me. Everything, EVERYTHING I'd been searching for, thirsting for, hungering for was in Him. All other pursuits were in vain. I'd embarked on a love affair with God! He had always been with me! He understood me, He wanted what was best for me and He KNEW what was best for me. He promised never to leave me or forsake me (Deuteronomy 31:6). He promised that whatever I experienced or suffered, whatever came my way, it would serve a greater purpose and He would use it for good (Romans 8:28). He gave me a purpose:

to know Him and love Him and love people the way He loved me, unconditionally, actively and generously. That's where I lost my step.

Michelle told me I needed to be in fellowship in order to walk this new path; I really did not want to. I would prefer to be a Christian by myself in my house with my Bible. Me and God. Solo mission for me. But, she insisted and being the people-pleaser I was, I let her drag me along. I reluctantly attended the Christian fellowship on campus; it was a struggle. When people asked me how I was doing, I did not know what to say. If I knew what they wanted me to say, then I would say that. When we would pray, I couldn't stop sizing them up and criticizing everything they prayed, which alienated me from them. When it was my turn to pray I was stressed because I was sure they were analyzing my prayers and judging me too. When we worshipped, I spent a lot of time thinking about my thoughts: "Why can't I stop lusting after that guy?! I'm such a creep." I could not shake those obsessive thoughts and would find myself bringing them back to God again and again, striving to be in the right state of mind; I could not relax.

They asked me to join a Bible study and I dreaded it every week. I remember telling them I couldn't get there until partway through and sometimes might not make it at all, so they changed the time for me! I still arrived late. One night, dreading it as usual, I procrastinated by spontaneously grocery shopping on my way there. When I arrived, the group decided to go on an outing and they asked me to drive! Since I did not have the courage to say "no," they got into my car and saw my fresh bags of groceries. I was found out. It was humiliating! My experience with people was riddled with embarrassing, awkward moments like that. I was just weird, selfish and dishonest. I didn't think of it as dishonesty because my intentions were good. I had to manage and control relationships and sometimes avoid them all together. At one point, a girl I lived near needed a ride to church on Sundays. Somehow I ended up being her designated driver and every week I had an excuse of why I couldn't make it, eventually neglecting to even call. I felt so overwhelmed and guilty about the situation; my solution was to change churches. It was just too much. So even though I wasn't drinking or doing the "bad things" I did before Christ (B.C.), this sense of shame, failure and demoralization haunted me. *It* still haunted me in my new life with Christ.

After a few attempts to drink "normally," I realized that for me to drink was to be drunk and painful consequences followed. Since I drank to get more and more of the effect, there was no point. I stopped drinking completely, but I was plagued by everything that drove the way I drank; I was perpetually uncomfortable. I was bound by my hamster-wheel thoughts, worries and fears. I constantly berated myself. Why didn't I feel the way I should feel? Why didn't I act right? I wanted to vanish into a movie. I would watch the same ones over and over and over again, wishing it could be my reality. I did not accept reality. Instead, I hid and pretended. I felt scared and alone whether I was by myself or in a room full of people, especially in a room full of people. B.C. it was alcohol that enabled me to enjoy social situations and without it, I was crawling out of my skin. This remained true even in the new Christian settings where I found myself. The drinking that I had done to cope was replaced by eating. I recall being at an overnight retreat and finding myself in this sea of college-age people who were connecting, laughing and talking. I was like a deer in headlights. When would it be time to go to bed? I vividly remember sitting by myself, quietly hoping nobody would notice that I was single-handedly downing an entire box of Oreo's. The Oreo's didn't give me the courage or the freedom that alcohol did, but it sort of took my mind off the people.

After Christ, family life was different. On one hand, I found myself relieved and grateful to have God with me in all the family situations and get-togethers. I would often go into the bathroom or an empty room and thank Him that He was there with me, that whatever was troubling me, I could bring it to Him and He would understand. But, I suddenly felt quiet and awkward around my siblings. They'd always gotten a kick out of me and adored my zany self. As a little girl, I'd taken on the role of entertainer and I would do anything to make them laugh. I performed. Now though, I was "weird" on the outside as well as the inside. I'd become serious and intense in my new-found faith.

I can recall a significant conversation with my sister, two years older than me. We were in my parents' office and she asked me, "What happened?" I used to be so fun, so silly and sassy. Now I was quiet, melancholy, isolated. It was devastating to me that she saw it that way. Coming to know Christ was the best thing that had ever happened to me! He was the first person to truly know me and the one person who I didn't have to fear finding me out and rejecting me. He saw all of me and covered me with grace. And my sister was telling me I'd taken a turn for the worse. I was angry because she was telling me that she wanted the old me back and the old me was a character, an actor, a façade. So the real me was a disappointment. I wanted to do it right, be enough, but I was totally mystified. I would try to connect with her and apparently say something awkward to find her looking back at me in disgust or annoyance. On the occasions I would go to social things with her I got the feeling I was an embarrassment and my perception of disapproval from her compounded my social anxiety. I felt inept, like the best I could do was keep my mouth shut. After a while I gave up.

In the next five years I took a rapid spiral down. The occasional slip into a food binge I'd experienced in college progressed into an all-consuming juggling act. I snapped like a rubber band between binging and starving. I could not eat normally. My life felt completely chaotic. I found myself out of the structure school had provided and I simply could not figure out how to live. If I'd still been drinking I would've been drowning by way of looking for an escape. Eating was the next best thing. I took solace in the planning and execution of binges. Ironically, these only contributed to my unmanageability, but for a brief period I would have a sense of control and gratification amidst feeling trapped by things that I had no control over. I felt overwhelmed by daily life. I don't know if it was depression or just an extreme lack of discipline, but it felt like the world was closing in on me. The things everyone else seemed to know how to do intuitively and even enjoyed doing baffled me. The things they enjoyed the most were the ones I dreaded the most: relationships and socializing. I just wanted to be left alone.

Early in the progression, I was willing to ask for help. I recall around this time hearing Scriptures such as, "man does not live on bread alone but on every word that comes from the mouth of the LORD," (Deuteronomy 8:3). I also heard a pastor teaching on the radio say that we are worshipping whatever it is that we spend the most time thinking about and get most excited about. I could not deny that what I got most excited about was food and what I thought the most about was my body and how I would lose weight. I didn't know what to do about it. I confided in a pastor at my church about my problem and he smiled good-naturedly and encouraged me to take it easy and to put the focus on my spirit rather than my flesh; like if I was sharing a meal with people, focus on them and our conversation rather than on the food. He said to spend time "feeding my spirit" through prayer and reading my Bible so that my spirit would grow strong and I would be guided by it rather than controlled by the desires of my flesh.

At times, I had no control. If I started eating I would not stop no matter how badly I wanted to, no matter how afraid I was of what I might be doing to my body. That fear fueled my frenzy, making it more necessary to continue. At times, my heart would race and my gut was telling me that I was putting myself in serious danger of a heart attack—from barely eating for days to eating three days' worth of calories in one sitting; occasionally throwing up or using laxatives, but usually launching into a period of starvation to make up for the binge. I'd felt that terror of powerlessness in the momentum of compulsive behavior throughout my life. It owned me. I was my abuser. I didn't want to feel the way *It* made me feel, but the compulsion was so strong, I could not fight it. The feelings that followed were not physical, but were more painful than the nausea of a hangover or any physical damage I'd done; it was shame, demoralization and hopelessness in the pit of my stomach; that is until the craving came back. With the craving came this manic feeling that this would be the last time and then I'd stop. Then I'd make a comeback, get past this and do all the things I dreamed about doing. I'd be the person I so badly wanted to be. But that hope and resolve only lasted until I found myself in the pit again.

My solution was to cut out any foods that I ate for any reason other than to nourish my body. I adopted a diet of vegetables, nuts, meat, eggs and occasionally fruit or whole grains, but only if I didn't get much pleasure out of it. My 5'8" frame went from about 150 lbs. down to about 110 lbs. in a matter of months, if not weeks. I loved it. Finally I wasn't chubby! I could finally stomach looking at my thighs. For once in my life, I did not feel like a pig. I felt worthy. I was really living the Christian life now, unlike all these hedonistic Christians around me. I wasn't even convinced they were saved. I knew I was because I had laid down my idols. It was exhilarating. All I wanted was God. I prayed constantly. I immersed myself in church, Bible study and prayer meetings. I didn't have to hide anymore because I didn't have anything to hide. I was a genuine Christian, practically a saint the way I was living. The only thing I guessed I needed to hide was my temper, how I felt, what I thought and anything you might not like about me. And, my relationships with my family. It wasn't very Christian of me to shout "F**king leave me alone!" when my phone would ring. And I wouldn't want anyone to know that I didn't know how to talk to my own family or that I criticized and judged everyone around me or that my word meant nothing because I never kept it.

At this point, people would attempt to help me, but I would not believe anything anybody said. I felt afraid to take their word for it and miss God's plan. For example I believed that if I didn't fast and eat this strict way, I would be disobedient and disqualify myself. At times, I was actually afraid of losing my salvation and questioned whether they actually knew God even though they thought they did. Ironically, they were reaching out to me in love and concern and I was in a total craze because I was so focused on myself I could not see. It told me that nobody can be trusted.

I was so afraid. Fear was the root and fruit of my thoughts and actions. I was afraid of misunderstanding God. I was afraid of not heeding these compulsive thoughts about food discipline and afraid that I'd never be able to stop lashing out in binges even if the consequences for me were eternity apart from God's love and goodness. Completely opposite things seemed true at the same time and I didn't know what way was the actual truth. For example I wondered if God was calling me to this extreme way of eating and if I didn't obey would I forfeit His will for my life and eventually fall away from Him? Or was I misunderstanding God and making the whole thing up? People suggested He wanted me to stop striving for perfection and that it was enough for me to just spend time with Him and love people, but that just seemed too simplistic. Besides, I didn't know how to be with people. My disordered eating took me further and further away from the simple truth of God's love and grace and deeper and deeper into the dark corners of my mind, constantly devising complicated formulas and plans for how I would get over this, how I would eat the way He wanted me to eat and be the person He wanted me to be. I walked on eggshells, feeling that the smallest decision was of paramount importance. I didn't feel free to do anything I wanted to do; in fact, I believed if I wanted to do it, it must not be God's will because God wanted sacrifice. I thought that I was called to deny my natural instincts in every way; that if I was willing to pray late into the night and read my Bible early in the morning, He would give me the energy and strength I needed to be at all of my divine appointments that day. I was convinced that every natural instinct that I had was my selfish, self-indulgent flesh and I must transcend it.

Besides my mom and sisters hounding me to put weight on, my boss and friend at the flower shop where I worked started commenting that I looked sick and it was hard to look at me. One day I had to leave work because I'd become so nauseated and shaky. I was convinced that God was calling me to a forty hour fast from water as well as food and as I tried to carry it out at work, I became dizzy and got sent home.

When I think about it now, it's so sad; to Him it must've been pitiful watching one of His creatures destroying herself in an effort to secure His love and protection. In hindsight, it's exactly the opposite of His way. Trusting in His love, in the sufficiency of His grace, accepting His forgiveness moment by moment and extending compassion to others, those would set me free from the bondage of self. I truly believe today that He only wants me to receive His love and respond with my love by serving others. I know today that He was loving me, encouraging me, wanting to help me as much in my ugliest moments of addiction as He does when I believe I'm at my best. I know now the same amount of His love and favor rests on me at all times, regardless of my thoughts, feelings or behavior. I can't get Him to stop loving me!

Eventually, my rigorous eating disciplines became punctuated with binges. I would eat some fatty decadent food and end up making a late night binge of it, going through multiple drive-through restaurants in a row, driving around late into the night eating and feeling like a complete lunatic. I would eat large portions of my parents' food overnight and wonder if they noticed, never saying anything about it. Sometimes the bingeing became so routine that I would lay in bed at night promising myself I wouldn't do it, only to succumb, getting out of bed and into my car for another shameful and vain quest for satisfaction. I felt so alone, crazy and out of control. Would I ever emerge from this cyclone?

I was in my early twenties and my life consisted of work, church and binge eating, veiled by a skinny frame, a perpetual smile and a knack for saying what people wanted to hear. I had bills that had gone to collections, even though I had a full time job and lived rent-free with my parents. I had no desire to be social. Although, I did have a crush . . . okay, an obsession with a guy in my church, but would never let on about it lest I be rejected. It had been years since I danced which had been my lifelong passion. I was surviving and felt I was failing miserably at living my life.

My mom, who was helplessly watching my struggle from a front row seat, eventually drew a boundary saying that if I did not get some kind of help, I could not continue living in her and my dad's house. She would like me to go to a treatment center for eating disorders, but I needed to at least start going to therapy. I felt that her suggestion that I go to an inpatient treatment program was ridiculous and melodramatic, so I agreed to get therapy. I had tried some different programs to get free of *It*, including an "As Seen on TV" kit for fighting anxiety and depression which I'd ordered while binging in front of late night television. I wasn't excited about it, but the idea of trying something new gave me a glimmer of hope. My mom and dad paid for me to see a therapist who was a total Godsend. She was a dynamic and practical Christian woman. I liked her. She said "f**k" once during a session and I laughed so hard she went on to weave profanity into our conversations saying that "cusswords weed out the legalists." I loved that. She told me things that were so radical to me, I had a hard time believing they were true like, "Your number one purpose is to be the happiest, healthiest person you can be." That sounded so selfish and self-indulgent. I was under the impression that any attempt to fulfill a desire was a sin and couldn't possibly be in line with God's will for me. I thought God's will was marked by self-sacrifice, ignoring self. I thought that saying "no" to a request was selfish—that's why I avoided people. I thought that trying to make something happen was being self-willed. She told me to "pray like it depends on God, but live like it depends on me." I thought listening to my gut was being in my flesh: she encouraged me to be honest about what my gut was telling me. She encouraged me to say "no" to most invitations and requests unless I sincerely wanted to say "yes," and that if anybody troubled me about it, simply admit that my limitations are disappointing and I can understand their displeasure, but still, "no." I could not accept most of her ideas and suggestions because I was very skeptical of their validity. Regarding food, she made various recommendations, none of which looked anything like my "plan." In hindsight, she talked very little about food and her suggestions for food were broad, as if food was not that important other than the priority of me not binge eating or starving. It didn't matter so much what I ate as long as I stayed out of shame.

I continued to struggle with my eating throughout and after my three years of therapy with Clare, although it became less pervasive in my life. I met and became engaged to my husband. In hindsight, his response to my eating disorder was a significant part of the healing process God has brought me through. My husband and I met at work. After we became acquainted, he started attending my church. One Sunday we sat together and he found me each Sunday after. Eventually we started talking on the phone, dated and within four months of dating were engaged. We were married nine months after that. Telling someone other than a therapist a little about my eating disorder was healing to me. And having someone who I love and respect laugh when I told them "I did it again" diffused a lot of the power out of my shame-driven food behaviors. However, I continued to have flare-ups, getting into cycles of binges, for days or weeks at a time and struggling to keep them secret. That didn't take so much of a toll on my husband and our marriage as the self-hatred and other "demons" that I and in turn, he, suffered from.

It pervaded our home, especially my volatile temper, emotional instability and self-centeredness. Now my husband and I were captive to my unpredictable moods and destructive attitudes and behavior. My husband encouraged me to seek some kind of help. I was willing. I submitted an anonymous prayer request on K-LOVE's website and returned to the twelve step meetings I'd attended in the past. I felt like kind of an intruder because I often identified more with the people the members were there to talk about, their family members and friends whose self-destructive behavior bothered them. But, there were a few people in the meetings that I looked forward to hearing because I related closely with them. The first meeting I attended, the person who led voiced the prayer I'd been praying for so long, "God save me from me." I was astonished and so comforted.

After one of the meetings, someone I especially related to invited me to attend a daily 6 a.m. meeting at their other program. I went because I could really use a meeting first thing in the morning and this meeting happened to welcome visitors. As I listened to people share, I experienced relief and hope; it was like I'd found my species. I found myself surrounded by lovable people I enjoyed and admired, who described an experience of life that matched my own. I heard "I hate myself and I'm all I think about," "Normal people don't become suicidal over a flat tire," "I'm an ego-maniac with an inferiority complex" and eventually, "If you have to control your drinking it might be out of control." As I listened to them, I identified with why and how they drank and my eyes opened to the fact that I was not a normal drinker. To enjoy my drinking was to not control it, and to control it meant not enjoying it. I couldn't have articulated it until then, but in the couple years I had started drinking at home with my husband, I felt frustrated, guilty and a little scared as I experienced that tension.

I'd prayed about my drinking once or twice as I sensed familiar feelings of obsession and compulsion creeping up. Then I reasoned that it was just my drinking history that made me uneasy and that with some practice, I'd learn how to control and enjoy my drinking. As I listened in the meetings, I recalled my own insanity not just from my early drinking career, but also recently. For example, one night I tottered through my house, feeling guilty about drinking more than I should have while deliberating on whether I could get away with having a little more, then calling the cops on my next door neighbors who were having a loud party because they were drinking way too much and someone needed to do something about the fact that "those ass-holes were out of control." I hadn't recognized that focusing on people who were worse than me was denial; they had the problem, they needed help. I'd started creating rules for myself, which I was not keeping, such as only drinking on weekends or only having it when my husband bought it for me rather than buying it for myself. But there was often a good reason to drink during the week and when I didn't buy it for myself I'd end up drinking some of his. I found myself once again feeling like a pig with alcohol—always wanting more, needing to justify why I deserved a drink at this moment or a little bit more than I intended. I was becoming self-conscious about drinking with my husband. I didn't want him to notice that I was chasing more of the effect or that when he poured more into his glass than mine it agitated me. These signs of abnormal drinking came to my attention as I listened to these people who'd earned my trust with their honesty, understanding and genuine compassion.

I heard some people say they believe they were born with this disease, that looking back they realized the day they walked into kindergarten, they "needed something," like a drink. I understood that! To be surrounded by people whose insides matched my insides was exhilarating! Not to mention seeing and hearing how they'd been able to change and how they didn't have to do those things anymore. I saw light in their eyes and joy on their faces. I observed people who were struggling to be honest about their situation and to keep showing up. They told me that even though I had not gone to the lengths of suffering and destruction they had, I was welcomed; that if I needed to do some more experimenting, have at it, but I would probably eventually end up back there after some consequences, if I was lucky. They told me to look for the similarities, rather than the differences. They told me I wasn't a bad person who needed to get good, I was a sick person that needed to get well. They said if I was willing to admit what the problem was, then I could do something about it.

By God's grace, I came to believe that I'm not unique, that I have a three-fold disease comprised of an allergy of the body, an obsession of the mind and a spiritual malady. God scooped me up and dropped me in this lifeboat before I'd realized the seriousness of my situation. I'd been praying in the other program for a woman who could take me through the steps, but didn't hear or see anyone who stood out. Within weeks of attending the meetings at my program, I found myself sitting next to a woman who looked my age with a confident and peaceful demeanor. After the meeting, I turned to bolt, but before I could get away she asked me about myself. She invited me to attend a women's meeting with her sometime and on a day when I was feeling particularly desperate, I called her and we went to the meeting.

During the car ride she told me about herself and her path. I related so much. But the confident, free woman I observed now didn't resemble the scared little girl she described. I thought if she could go from being the way she was then to the way she is now, maybe she could help me change too. I was struck by the sense that God had answered my prayer. If it wasn't so obvious, I probably would not have had the willingness or the courage to ask her to help me, but it was like the script had already been written and my next line was to ask. So I did and she said yes. Immediately, we went into action with her giving me assignments and me following her directions. I hated calling her; I didn't even answer my phone and she wanted me to call her every day? The feelings of vulnerability and the panic that followed were overwhelming at times, but the rewards were so profound, they drove me forward. Also, the ways I found myself changing gave me enough hope to know that I did not have to feel the way I'd always felt or act the ways I'd always acted. As I followed the path of the twelve steps under the direction of my sponsor, I began to change; my husband seemed less and less on edge around me and eventually even at ease. At work, I found myself less bitter and defensive and experienced joy in giving of myself. I began showing up for my family, eventually with a single motive to be useful or bless them somehow, which relieved me of the bondage of self-centered fear. God was doing for me what I could never do for myself!

It's been a hilly and winding road. At times I've come close to bailing out. He's brought me through painful periods of doubt, feelings of terminal uniqueness, the idea that I have a lot of drinking to do before I get sober, moments of believing, "I'm the same old me and I'll never change," weariness of being vulnerable and confusion as

I learn new ways of living. But God assures me that I am exactly where I am supposed to be and I am exactly who I am supposed to be at this moment. He "winks" at me through my Bible, my husband, my sponsor, fellow members, the TV, a movie, a billboard or a song; He spurs me on through their voice whether they realize it or not. At times the only thing that's kept me coming back has been the fear of reverting to my old miserable ways or doing something even worse. I believe that if I do what I always did, I'm going to get what I always got. I ended up here because I didn't want what I had, so I stay the course and come out on the other side.

Sobriety has brought so many wonderful gifts that I didn't think I wanted or believe I could ever have: enjoying friendship with people who know the good, bad and the ugly about me and love me as I am, the gift of being a true friend, the peace of believing that "all is well" even when I don't understand or don't like what's happening, feeling comfortable in my own skin and knowing how to act by focusing on how I can be helpful and trusting that God will guide me if I listen. He blesses me with the incredible JOY of being useful to a fellow human being because we share the same disease.

I feel God has brought me to my promised land. It has become the very thing that drives me to Himself and serves as the material for my relationships with other people who I relate to, love and enjoy. In this beautiful way of life, I am often satisfied and content. I am useful not in spite of, but because of, my disease. It is so unexpected, but isn't that God? The God of opposites: through death, we find life; He who knew no sin became sin! By confessing our neediness, we receive what we need in abundance. "When we are weak, then we are strong."

I can say with certainty that He is working all things together for my good. The vicious cycle of addiction has brought me to the freedom of knowing that I am entirely justified only by Christ's work on the cross on my behalf and He will not let me go. I always felt I was on the wrong planet and I was the only one of my kind; an alien. But today, I know I am not unique and my years of struggle and the solution that's been freely given to me are the very things I have to share with another human being.

Fourteen years ago, I was pacing the circumference of my parents' back yard late at night like a caged animal, wild with fear. I could not get away from myself. I can vividly recall kneeling and asking God, "Whatever is wrong with me, please remove it! I can't live like this. Please, take it out by the roots!" Today I am aware that

He has answered that prayer in a manner "immeasurably more than all we ask or imagine" (Ephesians 3:20). Having been free of a hopeless state of mind and body for two years and eleven months, I am filled with hope for the future. God gave me a manner of living that works. I believe that if for today I remain willing to trust God and walk the path of the twelve steps that has been laid out for me, I will continue to live and love with increasing peace and joy. I believe the best is yet to come. *"But I trust in you, O LORD; I say, 'You are my God.' My times are in your hands,"* (Psalm 31:14-15).

Lisa

"So do not fear, for I am with you; do not be dismayed, for I am your God. I will strengthen you and help you; I will uphold you with my righteous right hand."   Isaiah 41:10

My walls are full of pictures now; captured smiles that take me back to another time when he was here. My bookshelves brim with a variety of subjects; books that interest me, describe me, help me and captivate me. But there on the bottom shelf are the books on grief that I never set out to own.

My journal is full of yesterdays, those memories that have meant the most to me and have touched my heart in a special way. In it though, at one horrible entry, there exists an unwanted and invisible bookmark that separates my life into two chapters, "then" and "now."

Even though everything in my life seems okay now, tucked away in the recesses of my heart is a pain that may never go away. But, I have found that there is One who completely understands my broken mother's heart. *God has shown me that He alone is enough to bring me through anything that comes my way.*

His name was Anthony James Payne and I simply adored him. Being my first born son of five gave him a very special place in my heart. He was the first person that I ever loved more than life itself. He was the first person that I would have laid down my own life for in a heartbeat. I remember hearing his first cry after forty-two hours of hard labor. That beautiful sound moved me to tears. I remember gazing into his eyes for the first time and falling so completely in love with this precious child. I remember also feeling so afraid that I wouldn't be able to protect him from the sometimes cruel world that I had experienced. I remember thinking he was so perfect, so precious and so deserving of my very best that I vowed to give that to him. However being such a young mom, only seventeen when he was born, I made many mistakes during those early years. As I look back now though, I realize that those mistakes and the lessons that I learned from them, are what God used to mold me into the mom and the woman who He created me to be and for that I am grateful.

The role of mom, by far, has been my favorite. I can't think of any other area that I have learned so many valuable lessons about life. I learned unconditional love. I learned to pray fervently for those I deeply love. I learned to put others' needs before my own. I learned to have faith when things were tough and I learned to never stop believing in myself and more importantly, in God. I learned how to work hard and how to make time for fun. I learned when to say "yes" and when to say "no." I learned when to give in and when to stand firm for the things that I believe in. I have learned to treasure each day that I am given because life truly is a gift, each day an unrepeatable present that cannot be relived or regained once it is gone. I have learned to cherish the good times because I have also learned that life can change at any moment. It was Thursday, August 14th, 2008. I was sitting in the parking lot of Montclair Plaza reading the 23rd Psalm in preparation for a talk that I had been asked to give, when Anthony called. I almost didn't take that call because I was pouting over several conversations that we had earlier in the week.

Anthony called me on Monday to tell me that he was going to purchase a new motorcycle. Without hesitation, I drew my sword and hurled the weapon of words: "When you don't get that bike, you'll know it's because your mom is on her knees praying that God slams that door shut!"

"No Mom, don't pray that," he laughed as he quickly changed the subject.

We spoke again on Tuesday and several times on Wednesday. Each time I did my best to persuade him to reconsider; in fact, I begged him. Each time I failed.

Anthony and I enjoyed a very special mom/son relationship, which had really blossomed over the previous couple of years. As a young adult, just two weeks away from his twenty-fourth birthday, he was learning some incredible lessons about life. The beauty of it was that he shared some of the things that he was learning with me. I had learned earlier to bite my tongue when it came to offering my opinions or advice unless he asked for them. In doing this, it allowed us to become much closer. I found that he opened up his heart to me and shared the things that were important to him. He also shared his struggles. Instead of always trying to fix things for him, I listened and continually assured him that I would be praying for him, which he really seemed to value.

Part of my journey as Anthony's mom included going through years of his addiction problems, which started in his early teens. His addiction to methamphetamine had taken him down some dark paths, which were heartbreaking for me and yet God had taught me some incredible things during those years. He caused my faith to grow deeper as well as taught me to trust Him with the things that were beyond my ability to control or change. As I drew closer to Jesus and relied less on my efforts to fix my son, which were futile attempts anyway, God opened my eyes to the many ways that He was working in Anthony's life.

Anthony continued to grow in so many ways, especially after his twenty-second birthday. He was both active and passionate about his recovery from drug addiction and he found great hope and strength from attending Narcotics Anonymous meetings. Though he stumbled a few times, as many addicts often do, he never lost his determination. I felt confident that God indeed would give Anthony the complete victory over his addiction problem. I also loved that God used Anthony's relapses to teach him that he needed others on his journey of recovery.

Anthony sought out and found a sponsor that he spoke of often. He also tapped into the amazing resource that he had in my husband Gary, who twenty-two years earlier, had found victory over his drugs and alcoholism through his faith in Jesus and his attendance at Alcoholics Anonymous. I loved that Anthony called Gary often to talk through those difficult things that he was working through. I loved to listen to the laughter and words of encouragement and wisdom that Gary offered my son. I loved that Anthony truly respected and found the love of a father in my husband.

I was also excited about a special girl named Amber that Anthony had purchased a ring for. I use the words "purchased a ring" because Anthony had commitment issues; he never quite said, "We're getting married," but that too, I believed, would happen in time. Although Anthony and Amber had broken up two weeks prior to this time, it wasn't the first time they had called it quits and besides, they always seemed to work it out.

As I watched them together, it was evident that she loved him and I'm sure he loved her as well. As far as I could tell, the biggest problem for them was that Anthony was extremely strong and good looking and he was full of charisma, but he was also full of himself. Girls paid close attention to Anthony and he knew it. While Anthony loved causing heads to turn, Amber wasn't quite as enthused about it. During the times that they were broken up, Anthony's thoughts consumed him; "How do I smoothly get her back?"

I especially thought it was funny when he called me during this last break up to tell me that his best friend Kendall was making his move on Amber. Anthony was furious and asked me what I thought he should do about it. Since "he asked" for my opinion, I held nothing back. I told him, "Stop being an idiot and call her. Above all else, stop flirting with every pretty girl you meet." He agreed that he would. Of course there was one other reason that they had broken up in the past, but Anthony had been clean for quite some time so I didn't even consider that possibility.

Even though I had learned to restrain myself from giving Anthony my "motherly words of wisdom and advice" about other things, on the issue of the motorcycle, I felt very strongly the need to express my fear, whether he wanted to hear it or not. On Wednesday, I told him that I had a sickening feeling in the pit of my stomach about his decision to buy the bike. When that didn't work, I brought up the expense and how extremely irresponsible I thought he was being. He sharply said, "Look, I don't want to talk about it anymore." When we hung up the phone on Wednesday night, we were both agitated with each other.

On Thursday morning he called several times but I didn't answer his call because I was upset with him. I spent the day running some errands with my son Christian, who was fifteen at the time. Anthony was very close to all of his brothers. I loved the different relationships that he shared with them. He had a way of making them all feel special; like they were his favorite and they were. Christian and Anthony's bond was that they were so alike. I think Anthony saw himself in Christian. I loved to hear them laugh and share stories together. Anthony had a tattoo that said "Big Dawg." I loved to hear Christian brag about the times that Anthony called him "Little Dawg."

Throughout the afternoon, I could hear Christian as he talked with Anthony on the phone. This allowed me to know what things were going on in his day. "You're getting it today?" I heard Christian ask. "Cool, send me a picture of it." They were speaking of the motorcycle. Next was the phone call about lunch, "How long have you been waiting? Are you sure you're at the right Subway?" Anthony was waiting to have lunch with a girl who was late and he figured that she had probably stood him up. Later, through another phone call with Christian, I learned that he met that person for lunch and whoever she was, they had a fight. I didn't worry too much about it because I "knew" that later, when we were done being angry at each other, he would tell me all about it.

At exactly 7:00 p.m., Anthony sent Christian a picture of a red, high-powered Honda CR1000 known more commonly as a "crotch rocket." Christian showed me the picture and all I could do was shake my head in disapproval. Suddenly, as I was looking at the picture, Christian's phone rang. It was Anthony again. After Christian spoke with him a few minutes, I heard him say, "Dude, you're going to kill yourself on that thing." He was joking but I'm sure the thought entered his mind as it did mine. Christian put the phone down and said, "Come on Mom, he really wants to talk to you." I'm so glad I took that call.

I could hear the excitement in his voice when he said, "Hi Mom, did you see it?"

"Yes, Anthony, I saw the picture," I said.

"Do you like it?" he asked.

"No Anthony, I think it's the ugliest bike that I have ever seen and I hate it."

Anthony laughed. Anthony had always had such a charming and upbeat personality that it was virtually impossible to stay mad at him. When he was younger and insisted on getting into mischief with his younger brothers, he was the one that I went to first, partly because he was the oldest but mostly because I knew that he was the mastermind behind the stunts that they pulled together. He thought of things that no one thinks of.

On one occasion, when the boys were little, I opened my front door to our "less than friendly" neighbors, a couple who, on more than one occasion, came over to complain about my boy's shenanigans. The purpose of this visit was to inform me that someone had smeared jelly on the door knob of their house. The trick worked because the husband opened his hand to show me grape jelly all over the palm of his hand. Busted! Just moments before, I found spilled grape jelly all over the kitchen counter. I apologized profusely to my neighbors and assured them that the culprits would be over to apologize and to clean it up. I called out, "Anthony, get in here!" There was just something about that mischievous, half crooked smile of his that melted my heart. I offered him the same smile in return when I said, "That was a good one, Anthony. Now you march your behind over there and apologize and clean it up. Oh and Anthony, I want you to offer to mow their lawn for them this week." His smile quickly faded into a scowl. Though his charm made it hard to stay mad at him, on the issue of the motorcycle, it wasn't that I was really mad; I was just so afraid. I'm sure that he knew that.

After I told Anthony that I hated the bike, he laughed. "Come on Mom, it's going to be okay," he said.

"Anthony," I said seriously. "I know that there is nothing I can say that will keep you off of that bike. But please Anthony, please be very careful."

"Mom, I will," he reassured me.

I reiterated it. "Anthony, I'm very serious about this. We all love you very much and we are counting on having you around for a long time. I want for you to promise me that you'll be extra careful."

"Okay Mom. I promise you, I will be very careful." I heard his uncle talking in the background. Anthony abruptly and enthusiastically said, "Okay Mom, I've got to go now; we're taking it out for a ride. I'll call you later."

"Remember your promise Anthony. I love you."

"I love you too Mom." We hung up at 7:15. *I didn't have any idea that our conversation would be our last.*

I replay those words over and over again in my mind wishing that there were something I could have done differently. I wish I would have kept him on the phone longer. I wish I would have called his uncle to express my fears about this motorcycle. I wish I could have known that my fears would soon become a reality. Maybe then I would have tried harder and fought stronger so that he would still be here.

Carol Kent, in her book *A New Kind of Normal*, states, "At some point in our lives, most of us will face a faith test. It is that moment in time when what we have always believed about who God is and what He allows to happen in our lives intersects with the reality of our experiences; It's a head on collision between our faith and the hard facts of an impossible situation." My faith test came in the form of a phone call at 4:30 a.m.

It was a call that abruptly changed my life forever. The phone ringing in the middle of the night is not unusual in our home. My husband runs a ready mix company and often drivers or mechanics will call my husband's cell phone at all hours. This call however was not on my husband's cell. It was the house phone that was ringing, which was very unusual. I heard my husband answer quietly, "Hello, who is this?" Just as he always does when receiving a call when we are sleeping, he got up and went into the bathroom, closed the door and tried to talk quiet enough as to not disturb me. It didn't work.

I heard him ask, "Why are you crying? Slow down, I can't understand you. Why are you crying?" That question seemed to quickly lure me out of my drowsy state. I continued listening, "Amber, why are you crying, what's wrong?" Realizing that he was talking to Amber, my son's girlfriend, caused my heart to drop and now I was wide awake. Very adamantly he said, "Don't you say that Amber, don't you say that!" Just as he flung open the bathroom door and flipped on the lights, I tore the blankets from my body and I looked at Gary confusingly. With a look on his face that I have never seen before, all that he could whisper was, "Anthony." I slowly reached my hand out for him to give me the phone. I felt the resistance as he didn't want to let go of the phone.

I put the phone to my ear; I could hear her sobbing. "Amber, what's wrong? Where's Anthony?"

Her words were the words that every mom prays that she would never hear. "Lisa, he's gone. Anthony is gone." I knew what she meant, but I couldn't process it.

"What do you mean he's gone?"

"Lisa, Anthony was involved in a head-on collision last night on his motorcycle and he didn't make it."

I don't know if there are words that adequately describe how I felt in that moment. From a place deeper than I knew existed within my soul, a slow wailing groan began to rise. All that I could say was, "No, not Anthony, not my Anthony."

I looked into my husband's eyes, begging for him to say, "Lisa, it's just a bad dream." He didn't speak. He tried to hold me but I broke free from him. I could not come to grips with myself or with anything else. The mom in me felt like I had to do something, but really what could I do? I couldn't breathe, I couldn't think, I couldn't even stand up. I found my way into the bathroom thinking that I was going to be sick, but I couldn't even do that. I slid down the corner of my bathroom wall and began to sob, begging God with all that I had to please not let this be true. I remember saying, "He promised me that he would be careful. It can't be true because he promised me." From the floor in the corner of my bathroom, I glanced up to a devotional that sits on the shelf. I stood up to read the words from Isaiah 41:10. Dated August 14th, it read, "Fear not, for I am with you. Do not be dismayed. I am your God. I will strengthen you; I will help you; I will uphold you with my victorious right hand." I cannot tell you that reading that took my pain away, but I will say that like never before, I heard and recognized God's voice speaking to me and he called me by name: "I am here, Lisa. I will never, ever leave you." That brought a certain stillness and clarity for me that I will never forget.

Upon receiving that phone call, God began working immediately. Gary knew, in our complete brokenness, to call out for help from another who could be strong for us when we absolutely could not be. He called one of the most amazing ladies that I have ever known, my very best friend Vickie Manning. Within minutes, she was at my side praying for me and for my family. As the news traveled quickly, so did all of our amazing friends and family. Throughout the morning, our home was filled with those precious people that God has placed in our lives. Their love and comfort was so helpful during those early hours. As the morning wore on, so did the details of what happened.

At 8:00 that morning, Gary spoke to the coroner and learned that the driver of the car that hit my son had been arrested for drunk driving. Both she and her passenger were injured, but nothing life threatening. A drunk driver had killed my son. In a strange way, I remember feeling relieved, because I knew that it wasn't Anthony's fault. It wasn't that he didn't keep his promise to me; someone else killed him. At 10:00 that morning, my husband took another call from a Sheriff's investigator. He informed us that the girl that killed my son was also Anthony's ex-girlfriend, a girl named Melissa. They believed it was intentional and she was being held for murder. All that they knew at that point was that she and Anthony had lunch together and some sort of argument took place, which escalated as the day wore on. Also, there were witnesses that saw them arguing on the side of the road just seconds before the accident.

Melissa was a girl from Anthony's past. They dated a short time one year earlier. It was during a time when Anthony and Amber were broken up and it was also during a time that he wasn't doing very well in his recovery. Why was he with her again? Why would she kill him? How could anyone ever want to kill my son? It was all too big for me to piece together at that time; nevertheless, I tried to make some sort of sense, but nothing added up.

As the investigator asked many questions of us that morning, there was only one question that I had for him: "How did my son die?" He wouldn't answer my question but later told my husband who gently revealed to me the answer that I needed to know. My son was traveling west on a two-way highway in the mountains where he lived. Melissa, his ex-girlfriend, was traveling east. As my son attempted to pass her, the car she was driving veered over the double yellow lines into my son's lane and hit him. His right leg was torn off at the hip upon collision. Because he was traveling at a high rate of speed, probably 80 miles per hour, he was thrown 200 feet and slid an additional 200 feet on the rough mountain asphalt. Additionally, they added the horrific detail that his clothes were torn off completely upon impact. Although we would have to wait for the coroner's report, the cause of death was likely that my son bled to death, combined with injuries sustained by blunt force trauma. Like a jagged knife, those words ripped violently through my heart and yet as awful as they were, I couldn't seem to stop replaying them over and over again in my mind.

With each new detail and change, there was also a new range of emotions and questions that were very difficult for me to process. There were times that I questioned God, saying, "How could you let this happen? Why would you take my son from me when he was just beginning to live?" Perhaps one of the most difficult realities for me was when I realized that my prayer life for my son Anthony had suddenly come to an end. How does a mom come to grips with something like that? The magnitude of losing my son was something that affected my life on every level. In a single moment, my life fell to pieces.

I felt like everything that I had ever believed about Jesus, every word that I have ever spoken, every verse from the Bible that I had ever read, every single thread of my professed faith, had been rocked to the core. I felt as though I had been hurled into deep and roaring seas of unfamiliar and gut-wrenching pain and either I would be swallowed up and drown, or Jesus would be my lifeline. It was completely up to Him because for the first time in my life, I felt stripped of every ounce of self-determination and strength. Yet, it also became very clear to me that the very second I began to question God in all of this—at that exact moment—He revealed His unquestionable love and presence in ways that I had never experienced before.

Before losing my son, I always said that I had strength to do many things, but losing a child is something that I could never get through. It is true; I alone, in my own strength, could never stand up under such gripping and heart wrenching pain. *The only explanation is that Jesus was and continues to be enough for me.*

The days and months ahead seemed to be unbearable at times, but somehow God always provided exactly what I needed. Not only did I have the task of burying my son, but also there were court proceedings and eventually the trial. Many well-meaning friends tried to persuade me to not attend the hearings. They thought maybe I would be able to find closure sooner, but the truth is I looked forward to those dates. As long as there was one more proceeding to attend, there was something to look forward to. I kept thinking that at some point, we would receive justice or something good would happen. It never did, at least not through the court hearings.

For the first seven months, the girl who killed my son was held in a small county jail facing a murder charge. The case seemed very strong and the newspapers as well as the local news channels reported that it would be a "slam-dunk" case. That wasn't the way it happened at all.

In April of 2009, just eight months after my son was killed, I received a call from the district attorney informing me that they had decided to drop the murder charge. Apparently, because Melissa was so intoxicated while driving, they didn't think they could prove beyond a shadow of a doubt that it was intentional. The evidence of witnesses who saw them arguing on the side of the road apparently was not enough to sustain a murder count. The fact that there were very angry and threatening texts being sent to my son's cell phone from Melissa was "suddenly" not persuasive enough either. I couldn't understand what was happening at all.

Because they dropped the murder count, they also released her from jail. My husband and I drove up to meet with the District Attorney. I was furious and someone needed to make sense of all of this for me. We were told that the events of that day, everything that took place between Melissa and Anthony, all served together to create the "perfect storm."

"What are you talking about?" I questioned in disgust and disbelief. I felt like the DA was dramatizing my son's death and even going as far as giving it a title from a popular movie. He infuriated me and did nothing to satisfy the questions for which I demanded answers, but never got.

I did learn however that a blood toxicology test revealed that my son had very small traces of methamphetamines in his blood. The low levels indicated that he would have used several days before the crash but not on that day. I later learned that Anthony had relapsed in his addiction two weeks prior to his death, which explained why he was back in touch with Melissa. I learned that his relapse was also part of the reason that he and Amber had broken up again.

Apparently Anthony had contacted Melissa right after he and Amber broke up and they resumed their dating relationship. I believe that for Melissa it was "true love," as her testimony later in court was that she loved Anthony and wanted to have his children. Yet for Anthony, it was nothing more than pretty company. Anthony had lunch with Melissa that day and the argument was over the fact that Anthony was calling it quits. His intention was to work things out with Amber, which infuriated Melissa.

After their fight at Subway, Melissa returned to work. After work she bought beer and drove to her friend's house and proceeded to get drunk. While she drank with her friend, there were very angry and sometimes threatening texts that were sent from Melissa to my son's phone. At some point, Melissa and her friend left the house to go to a party at another friend's house. It was at that exact time that my son was test driving his motorcycle, which had been purchased only one hour prior, on the back road that both he and Melissa were familiar with.

Apparently, Melissa saw Anthony on his motorcycle and they both pulled over to exchange words. There were witnesses that saw them arguing, but no one saw the exact impact of the collision. The district attorney told me again that the events that followed created the "perfect storm" of alcohol, drugs and anger. What the DA called a "perfect storm" was what I called murder. I felt like I was stuck in a terrible bad dream and that only my husband and I were able to see the insanity that was taking place.

Additionally, the defense attorney posed the scenario in his reports that perhaps Anthony had struck Melissa's car, which of course could have happened except for the evidence that Melissa's tires, all four of them, were completely in Anthony's lane. My husband was convinced that it all had to do with the budget cuts that were going on. My son's case was very expensive, as both the prosecutors and defense brought in their own accident recreation and reconstruction teams.

Additionally, there was another very public and high profile kidnapping case taking place in the same courtroom. My husband, along with others, believed that the decision to drop the murder charge against Melissa involved the necessity to free up money to fully prosecute this other high profile case. I, on the other hand, believed that it was due to the fact that my son had traces of drugs in his system and therefore, the zeal to prosecute that was there in the beginning was gone. Perhaps it was both reasons. Whatever the reasons were, I felt so frustrated and helpless because there was truly nothing I could do about it. Everything that I had prayed would not happen is exactly what did happen.

By the time we went to trial, almost two years had passed. The charges were reduced to Gross Vehicular Manslaughter with a special allegation of causing great bodily harm or death. The second count and less serious was Felony DUI. After two weeks of testimony and three days of deliberations, the trial ended in a hung jury. In order for a conviction, there has to be a unanimous vote. The only charge she was convicted of was felony DUI causing great bodily harm and/or death, which carries a two year prison sentence. She had already served half of that time so she went back to jail for an additional seven months. Nothing seemed fair at all, nor did it make any sense. I felt like I was stuck in the middle of a bad dream.

I cried myself to sleep so many nights those first couple of years. I just kept thinking at some point I would wake up and find that my life was still the same as it used to be. I think the desperation I felt was that I so badly wanted to go back to my old life, the way it was before August 14, 2008. I wanted to see my husband and children laugh again like we did before that phone call came. I wanted to enjoy the moment without that stabbing pain in my heart. I wanted to fall asleep at night without thinking about my son's final moments. I wanted most of all for Jesus to come back and take us all home where Anthony was. I begged God to give me a dream where I could see and talk to my son. At times I never wanted to get out of bed, but all the while, there was such a strong awareness that I was not alone and someone was carrying me. I kept sensing His still small voice saying, "I am enough for you." The truth is that when it all fell apart, He was enough and He carried me through each and every painful step of the way. Not only was He enough when it all fell apart, but He was also enough and able to make something beautiful out of my brokenness.

Ken Gire, in *The North Face of God*, writes, "When suffering shatters the carefully kept vase that is our lives, God stoops to pick up the pieces. But He doesn't put them back together again as a restoration project patterned after our former selves. Instead, He sifts through the rubble and selects some of the shards as raw material for another project-a mosaic that tells the story of redemption."

As I write this, it has been four years since I lost my precious son. While my heart still aches and I miss him greatly, I have seen the many ways that Jesus is taking the broken pieces of my life and He is putting them back together again in new ways.

Because of Jesus, I am stronger in my faith. My journey of loss includes so many things that I may never understand this side of Heaven. Faith, according to the Bible, is being sure of what we hope for and certain of what we do not see. As of now, I do not know all of the reasons that God allowed my son's life here to end. Yet, God in all of His mercy has allowed me to keeping moving forward, even when I don't understand. He has also given me many opportunities to offer encouragement to others along the way.

Before losing my son, I had no idea how to reach out to others who were in the deep valley of grief. Grieving is undeniably painful and God desires to use our experiences to help others on this journey. It has been such a blessing for me to encourage others, especially moms who may feel there is no hope or reason to go on since losing their child. Because I've been through this valley, I can honestly and confidently say that there is hope. Our hope is not in this world, but in Jesus. He is enough to bring us through and He will. The Bible says that Jesus is closest to the broken hearted and saves those who are crushed in spirit. It is not a cliché. It is a promise that I have experienced and found to be true.

Another way that I see Jesus taking the broken pieces of my life and creating something beautiful is that my family is so much closer now. Together, we have experienced something so painful and so tragic that I think we all recognize what is important in life. That doesn't mean we don't experience problems, because we do, but our love for each other seems to bring us through whatever comes our way. Divorce rates are very high when a couple loses a child, but it has been my experience that when a couple trudges the winding path of grief together, when they make the commitment and decision to stick together and tightly hold on to each other and to God, no matter how hard it may be at times. When the cloud begins to lift, the marriage and the family unit will be so much stronger.

Since Anthony's death, I have made it my goal to search for the good things that God may be doing through our loss. My husband and I have always been passionate about recovery and my life's mission statement is to bring hope to those whose lives are shattered by addiction. I have a feeling that the enemy thought that the death of my precious son would cause me to turn my back on Jesus. How very wrong he was. My son's death has actually allowed me to passionately offer hope to others who struggle with addiction. Both Gary and I serve in the ministries of *Celebrate Recovery* and *Teen Challenge*. Both programs are faith based programs that introduce people to the power, love and hope of Jesus Christ. This has brought me more joy than I could ever imagine.

Another blessing that I can see God working to bring about something good as a result of my son's death is through World Vision. I've always wanted to have a little girl, but God blessed me with sons (whom I would never trade). When Anthony died, I found myself feeling so sad on holidays like Christmas and especially on Anthony birthday, August 31st. One year I decided that even though I couldn't share these days with Anthony, I could intentionally share these days with another in Anthony's honor. For every year that Anthony has been away from me in Heaven, I have adopted a child through World Vision. Each child shares Anthony's birth date and each child so far, interestingly, has been a girl. In the time since Anthony has been gone, I have sponsored five children through World Vision. This has brought my heart much joy as Anthony's memory lives on in the lives of others.

Recently my son Shawn wrote in a college essay that "life can be difficult and tragedy can strike without warning, yet for those who walk with Jesus, there will also be a great opportunity to gain a higher trust, a deeper faith and a new-found purpose in our lives. I truly believe that God would not allow us to go through the painful valleys of our lives without having full intentions of using them for His glory and for His plan."

If you were to ask me now what I want more than anything else in the world, I would tell you that I want my son back here with me where he belongs. But somehow, I believe that at the end of my life, when I look back over what God has done and accomplished through losing my son, my thought is that I would say, I *wouldn't trade it for anything.*

Cherie

When I was four, I crawled into my parent's bed early one morning. I remember staring at the ceiling. My dad wrapped his arm tightly around me and I squirmed to free myself. A familiar battle ensued. I wanted to get up and play on that Saturday morning. My parents wanted to sleep in. I felt trapped and was unable to free myself from my father's grip. But my dad knew better than to let me go. I was a rambunctious, passionate, four-year old red head, who had left the house on several occasions to seek adventures.

My adventure seeking finally resulted in extreme measures. After leaving one time in the middle of the night to be returned by the police to very embarrassed parents, I was introduced to "The Harness." The harness was fitted to my twin bed and was safety pinned in the back to prevent me from leaving the bed. I fought against it many nights.

My personality was such that even as a small child, I believed in "leap first, look second." In spite of my lively nature, I had a very happy early childhood under the careful supervision of my parents. I remember playing hide and go seek until the street lights came on. Then there was kicking around in Marty Renick's backyard full of dirt hills. It was a great place for cowboys and Indians. Since my mother was a teacher, we were able to spend summers camping in the San Bernardino Mountains. My father, an insurance salesman, would join us on the weekends at the campground. My sisters and I rode bikes, hiked and swam at Jenks Lake. We played cards and board games with friends we met in the campground.

We moved to South Orange County the summer before fifth grade. I was mesmerized by all the kids running around in green and gold speedos at the clubhouse in the new 'hood. I begged my mom to let me join the swim team. My swim mates became my new group of friends. We trained in the mornings then played sharks and minnows for hours. We rode our bikes to the liquor store and would buy handfuls of candy. We would ride home and watch sitcoms, or take the bus to the beach, returning for afternoon practice. Life was fabulous. I had many friends and plenty of things to do.

Then, when I was fifteen, things changed. One day, my dad approached me with tears in his eyes. I had not seen my father cry up to that point. The memory is still vivid. He announced he would be leaving.

My parents' divorce when I was fifteen years old meant that my life no longer felt safe. My father married the woman with whom he had an affair and two of my swim team mates became my stepsisters.

I don't think it was the pain of the divorce, but my father's repeated choices, that indicated he cared more for his new wife and family than my sisters and me. Romance distracted my father and the single parenthood experience stunned my mother.

Looking back with my adult eyes, there were many indicators that my parents' marriage was in trouble. I still can picture a book titled *Open Marriage* I found in my parents' bathroom. I learned later that "Swinger Parties" were common in that era in my seemingly happy town.

My older sister was basically pushed out of the nest to marry at 18 before my parent's divorce would cause a scene. My younger sister and I stumbled through our teenage years. I felt abandoned by the father who repeatedly chose to spend time with his girlfriend and my future step-mother rather than be available for my sister and me when we needed a father's affirmation the most. I would carry the burden of my father's abandonment into many future relationships.

I managed to pick the guys that fit comfortably into this pattern. Either I wasn't attracted to the nice guy or I was too attracted to the emotionally unavailable guy. My identity was formed by the boys and men in my life. I was driven to prove I was attractive. I fought hard to win the affection of men. Ironically, this desperation sent men running and reinforced the lie of the enemy of my soul. I went into agreement with this lie and I felt undervalued and unseen. I became resigned and anticipated that the initial attention I received from men would not go the distance. I lost hope and I stopped expecting. I thought this strategy would prevent the pain of suffering from an unfulfilled expectation.

In high school, church was a refuge and provided me with youth leaders that loved and poured into me. Soon, I had a close relationship with God. I worked two summers at a Christian camp and remained involved in the college ministry at church. Despite this, my spiritual roots were not deep enough to sustain me through my college years.

I met my first husband while working as a waitress at a retirement community in South Orange County. He was an attendant for one of the residents. I was twenty years old, attending junior college and he was a thirty-four-year-old hippie, living in a beach town and pursuing a massage therapy certificate. He seemed to have a lifetime of experience compared to my limited innocent high school dating. He pursued me, but I declined to date him for months. Finally, after months of aggressive pursuit, I relented and agreed to date him. His Bohemian lifestyle appealed to my creative, adventurous side. I also enjoyed feeling a sense of belonging, as it seemed everyone in town called my boyfriend "Doc." When we became physically involved, I felt too incongruent to remain with my Christian walk.

I was able to move away to college to pursue a degree, but I was lonely and isolated from Christians. I would return home on long weekends and between semesters. I don't remember seeing or hearing much from my father during those times. I was however, very close to my mother and would begin missing her even before I would leave to return to school. My mother's home was full of joy and laughter. Her love blanketed me. I continued to date "Doc" and I decided to marry him in an attempt to justify the fact that I had given him my virginity. Now, I know now that God's grace and Christ dying on the cross was the only thing that could justify my sin.

Thankfully, my Heavenly Father still had His hand of protection on me as I did complete college and move into a viable career, which God would use to provide for me in very lean times.

While in college, I was very busy and seemingly happy. I worked thirty-two hours a week as a waitress at a Bob's Big Boy restaurant and carried a full academic load. I was vice president, then president, of my department. I enjoyed my college peers and the social life. The marriage, I am sure, kept me from the distraction of dating and allowed me to focus on my studies. Life was very scheduled between work, school and home. I loved my major. I loved being with my best friend and classmates.

One day, while in my senior year, a pair of psychology students came into a class I was taking. They were recruiting students to be "patients" in order to gain experience in their counseling. I thought this would be an interesting opportunity and I loved the psychology classes I was taking. I signed up. After the first appointment, I was referred to "The Professionals" who were the supervising teachers. After a few sessions, I realized my marriage had some problems. My husband had some serious emotional wounding from serving as a medic in the Vietnam War. We would later come to know this phenomenon as Post Traumatic Stress Disorder. He was addicted to marijuana and not really working. I hadn't really noticed as my life seemed so busy. My awareness began to crystalize when he crashed my car for the second time, forcing me to take public transportation. With increased financial stress, he was becoming critical of me and our verbal exchanges were beginning to get physical. When school was over, I decided to spend time with my family in Southern California to get perspective. I never returned and my mother and stepfather assisted me in obtaining a divorce.

I delayed my first internship and lived at my mother and stepfather's home. I worked a split shift at a chiropractor's office and took a "time-out" from the hectic pace I kept while attending college. I remember being in a complete fog for those few months, but time required me to get back on track. I began my first internship in Palm Springs at the end of the summer. I barely took time to get out of the daze and did not really get further help for my much needed healing. I was also walking far from God.

I moved to a condo provided by the hospital where I worked and life took off again. I was on a huge learning curve and worked hard during the week. On the weekends, I escaped in the bar scene with my roommates.

I met my second husband in Palm Springs, where I was completing my first internship. He was in Indio to play polo. His biceps below the crease of his linen shirt caught my eye on the dance floor. He drove a Porsche so I figured financial struggles would not be an issue with him. I did not ever want to suffer such financial hardship again. As with my first husband, there were parts of him that attracted my rambunctious side. He spoke French fluently, dressed in Italian clothes and introduced me to what I thought were the finer things in life.

I finished my internship and moved into a beach bungalow in Laguna. The place was small. Anyone taller than six feet would have to duck to enter and then would have to sit down right away. It was like living in a medium sized motorhome, but it was my home and I loved having my own place. The best part was being able to hear the waves at night as I fell asleep. I worked my first job and was back home on the sand by 4:00 p.m. each day. Though I did not live with my mother, I spent a great deal of time at her home as my stepfather had developed lung cancer and the doctors diagnosed him as terminally ill.

Walking through my stepfather's illness and eventual death at home was my introduction to suffering. I learned the importance of having family to just be present. It was then that I became acquainted with hospice care. Nurses would go to my mother and stepfather's home and provide comfort and emotional support, while my stepfather's life slipped away. It was a very painful illness and he required morphine to tolerate even lying in bed and breathing. He tried not to use the morphine, as it would rob him from being with us. It was a precarious tightrope he navigated as he balanced pain management with lucid thinking and speaking. He was either in excruciating pain as he expressed his love and desires for our future, or he was in a medication-induced coma.

During this time, I continued to date the desert polo player. He was moody and his attention vacillated. Our relationship was characterized by tumultuous breakups and reunions for ten years. By his own words, he was a committed bachelor. What does that mean? A desire for a close relationship without the risk of commitment? I was determined to heal his broken heart from all the failed attempts at intimacy he had in the past. If you have read the book *How We Love* by Milan and Kay Yerkovich, you would recognize my attachment style as the pleaser and those I dated as vacillators. When I stopped pursuing them and pulled away, they would pursue me.

This did not go so well most of the time. I experienced intermittent nice boyfriends when not dating him. I also experienced further wounding from the rejection I experienced. We would get close, then something would happen to mess it all up. One time, one of his old girlfriends from Paris surfaced in California. When I found a Cosmopolitan magazine on the nightstand next to his bed, I realized it was a planned vacation at my boyfriend's home. He was not being upfront. I tried to prove my attractiveness and slap a Band-Aid on my own pain by having one-night stands, which I thought would turn into relationships. Years of this tit-for-tat pattern followed and I suffered even deeper wounding.

I moved to a two bedroom condo with a girlfriend I had met through some self-improvement and communication classes. The technology from the workshops was helpful in some situations. I did learn how to communicate truth effectively and deepen relationships in the work setting. The technology was harmful though too, as it suggested I was in control of my destiny, rather than encouraging me to let God guide and direct my path. I was a young, single, professional woman. My roommate and I threw dinner parties and went to expensive restaurants and clubs every weekend. I continued my on and off relationship with the polo player. I believed the lie of the woman's movement that said sexual expression would lead to more liberty, but instead I felt myself dying. I no longer experienced the joy of my earlier years and I began to deny my own desires in order to please the desert bachelor. I lost who I was and who God had created me to be. I continued to be far from my path with God.

After my stepfather had passed away, my mother moved to a dream home in Huntington Beach. My mother had an eye for colors and design and her home looked like a model home. As she decorated her home, she began having what we thought were panic attacks. We thought the loss of her husband and the move was too much stress at one time. Later, we would learn she was actually having seizures. This came to light when she was found unconscious on the floor. The white carpet was red from the blood that had spilled from a gash on her head when she experienced a grand mal seizure. Tests soon revealed my mother had a brain tumor.

My roommate was moving back to her home in the Bay Area. Since I was the only sibling without a family of my own, I moved in to care for my mother. Soon, I had switched roles with my mother. At twenty-six, I was caring for her and making financial and medical decisions, along with my sisters and aunt. I was exhausted from working during the day and meeting her needs at night. Our extended family circled around to provide emotional and logistical support as we went to medical appointments. We even flew from Southern California to the San Francisco Bay area so that she could participate in a research study. Her tumor was aggressive and this research involvement allowed her to get the best available care.

Walking through my mother's illness was the most difficult experience in my life. After half a year of going back and forth to San Francisco, my sisters and I listened to an early recording of the first appointment with her doctors. It did not register the first time we heard it (professionals call it the denial stage of grief), but we heard it then. He had given her a very grave prognosis of less than a year to live. At this point we had only months left. She had gained weight from the steroids and now was seizing several times a day. One time, she had a seizure on the powered walkway at the airport. We could not get off the walkway until we reached the end. It was a very sad and terrifying moment. It was also a moment of truth. She could no longer tolerate these flights to San Francisco. We began to move into the acceptance phase of grief. We tried to make the most of each moment we had left with her.

My mother lost her hair from the chemotherapy. She was brave, though, and did not let these physical losses steal her joy. She used her new hairstyle as an excuse to act on her hat obsession. She hired a personal shopper and began her shopping binge. She bought Diane von Furstenberg dresses and hats to go with each new outfit. I think she was making up for her earlier frugal years. She soon became dependent on a wheelchair, but this did not keep her from social engagements. She even went to a couple of reggae clubs with me and my friends. She did not lose her sense of humor and this proved to be a great gift as she adjusted to the many losses.

Unlike my stepfather's course, my mother did not suffer from pain. There are no pain receptors deep within the brain. Despite this, the emotions we experienced together were raw, deep and varied within each hour. Together, we grieved her loss of independence and future. We laughed at the daily challenges that presented themselves. One time, when transferring from the bathtub to her wheelchair, she slipped slowly to the floor. We could not support her weight and had to lower her to the floor. The worst part was we had to get the neighbor to help us. We did cover her with a blanket, but a slippery heavy body was difficult to move. We laughed at the neighbor's reaction once he left the house.

My mother would get confused and reality would blur with television shows she watched. She loved the shopping network and we never knew what sort of package might mysteriously appear on the front porch. We continued to receive packages even after her death. My sisters and I just laughed at what she "couldn't live without." She was famous for the middle of the night requests made through the baby monitor we used. "Scooby Snacks" became a regular occurrence.

In lucid times, I had the opportunity to ask her about events in my life that didn't make sense to me growing up. She spoke truthfully and we had the opportunity to learn things we may not have learned under different circumstances. I was also privileged to become acquainted with her brilliance as a teacher. By what she had shared in earlier years, I was under the impression she was not liked in the work place due to her eccentric personality. She was a kindergarten teacher by day and transformed into a belly dancer at night. She enjoyed dancing at various venues while my stepfather played the Middle Eastern drum. She had several projects at school, which landed her the Golden Apple award for the state of California. She thought her coworkers were jealous of her winning this prestigious honor.

As God always does, He turned that which was meant for destruction into something good. This illness was a gift. My mother learned that she was loved deeply. Teachers came by twos and threes to visit her every day. Her children had the opportunity to understand and know her better through their stories.

As our journey came to an end, I was depleted of emotions. I had cried all I could cry. I had been as stressed out as I could possibly be stressed. (I had three occasions where I had rear ended cars on the freeway on my way to work. Surprisingly, there was no damage noted upon a road side inspection). In this void, I experienced something I had not experienced previously. I had a deep sense of love for everyone in my life. I even loved those who I thought were my enemies. The veil of relationship misperception dropped and truth invaded almost every area in my life. But, I still did not realize how far I was from God.

My life resumed and I moved into an apartment and picked up where I had left off with the polo player. On one of our reunions, I became pregnant with my now seventeen-year-old daughter. We continued a pattern of living apart then getting back together. We moved in together then separated. I was able to buy a beautiful condo in Dana Point (with my inheritance) and had moved my way up the career ladder to a hospital administrator position. Single parenthood was very stressful. Soon the polo player proposed. He told me if he could just do what he loved to do, we would have a happy marriage. So, when my daughter was three, I sold my ocean view condo and resigned an executive position in a hospital. We married and moved to a forty-acre ranch in Houston so that he could pursue his love of horses. It sounded like a dream to many of my coworkers and supervisors in key positions at the hospital. It was exciting and wonderful for about a month. Then there was a delay in getting my license in the state of Texas and he began pressuring me to make money.

Once I did get my license, I had to travel long distances to treat in a variety of settings. When I would return home from a long day, my husband expected me to prepare dinner, clean up and get our daughter ready for bed. One night, this chronic people-pleaser had an "aha" moment. I unsuccessfully fought back tears as I read a bedtime story to our young daughter. I was on the hamster wheel again, working hard to keep life moving forward.

There were moments of happiness, but again I found myself isolated from friends and family and the only one bringing income into the household. How had I created the exact situation of my first marriage? Only this time there was a third innocent life to consider. My husband moved to the inner loop in Houston to find work. I continued to work in the rural community. We had to sell the farm and my daughter and I joined my husband in Houston. I did not realize how depressed I was until I went for an annual checkup and could not stop crying. As I sat in the doctor's office, I kept picturing a faucet like one outside my home. I kept telling myself, "Just turn it off." I could not. I could not stop crying. I was referred again to a counselor for help. My husband and I went to marriage counseling for a few months, but we were unsuccessful in trying to find someone with whom we both could click. Either the counselor "sided" with him or "sided" with me.

Confronted with evidence of my husband's infidelity, I moved out of our home. My daughter and I went to live with generous and kind co-workers. They had an extra room and it gave us time to "re-group." They bought me a round trip ticket to visit my dad and stepmother for Thanksgiving. I missed my mother and her love for me deeply. I wished she were still alive to impart her wisdom to me and love me through this difficult time. Instead, I was met with my dad and stepmother's perception of, "Oh, all marriages go through this and it will get better." I knew there was no getting better as all attempts at marriage counseling had failed. I wish now that I had Godly people in my life who could have encouraged me and mentored me in God's divine plan for marriage. I was experiencing the high cost of living outside of God's protection.

When I returned to Houston, I found out I was pregnant again, but the joy was squelched by the discovery my husband was continuing to be sexually active outside our marriage vows. When my son was one month old, I returned to Southern California. I told my husband his family would be waiting for him in California when he was ready to be a married man. It was a very difficult time. I had to find work, a place to live and a workable childcare situation. Though my sister said I could stay with her, I knew that it would be very temporary as she had a full sized family of her own.

I soon learned God would meet every need beyond that which I could even imagine. I began going to Saddleback Church and God began rebuilding my life as I stepped out in faith. Someone close to me had friends looking for tenants. It was a very reasonably priced three bedroom with a yard and attached garage. It was affordable and freeway close, yet tucked into the hillside so traffic was minimal. It was a safe place to bring my children. I soon received another blessing of having a household of furniture for the cost of a U-Haul in order to move it to my new place.

The father of my children did eventually follow us out to California and we experienced some intermittent happiness, but despite my frequent requests, the truth of the affairs was not brought into the light for healing to occur in our marriage. He refused counseling and we continued to have problems. He was depressed, addicted to marijuana, unemployed and angry that I had become so involved in the church. When the topic of separating one more time came up, he said "No more separations. I want a divorce."

God had blessed me with a good income and then an opportunity to start my own business. I was able to buy my husband out of the house and ironically owed him more spousal support than he owed me child support. I had been in counseling since my return to California and had experienced much healing through Christian counseling and through programs the church offered. I was involved in small groups and felt pretty well prepared for single parenthood. I had been through many separations and I had peace as there was no longer a need to play detective and question my sanity. I was healing. My beauty was beginning to be revealed. My laughter was attractive and I soon found myself in an unexpected predicament. I was "Forty-seven going on Seventeen" (a chapter title from the book *Growing through Divorce*) and ill prepared for the unexpected attention from men.

I was well plugged-in at a mega-church, but was exhausted from trying to be a single parent and start a new business. I was also assuming the management of my personal finances and making sure the kids got their chores and homework completed, as those were roles my husband did well in the marriage. I was broke and exhausted. One Friday in December, I decided it would be a good idea to go to the community clubhouse holiday party. I reasoned that my children and I would have fun and dinner would be free. Tables were filled with clubhouse party foods like cubed cheddar cheese, salami and Ritz™ crackers. The kids in the community were running amuck and my children weren't ready to leave. I noticed some of the parents walking down from the bar area with cocktails. I decided to follow the other parents' leads and go to the Friday Bar and grab a beer to unwind.

As I sat and pondered all the things on my "To do" list, I sipped, well more accurately, guzzled a Corona. I didn't make it downstairs before a young hunk said, "Hey why don't you run your errands and return?" I said "Probably not," as I was exhausted and had so much to do, but "Thanks anyway."

Later, while wrestling with my shopping list and budget, I thought about the encounter in the bar. "Why not? It could be fun and quite a nice break from this monotony of single parenthood." Again, I did not recognize the lie I was beginning to buy into. It was a lie because my life was anything but monotonous. God had been meeting me at every step as I was beginning to walk with Him. God was still with me, if I only would take the time to see Him.

Then it happened. This rambunctious wounded girl began the relationship I would equate to the experience of wiping out at the beach. You know the feeling if you ever lived on the Pacific Coast: the struggle to shore in order to preserve life, followed by the need to take inventory. There would be damage caused by the combination of the powerful waves, hard ocean floor and my soft body.

This guy from Hawaii was seven years younger than me and very charismatic. I was surprised and flattered that he found this old, exhausted girl attractive. He said he was a Christian. At that moment, that was good enough for me. Later, I would learn you have to examine the fruit of the walk. He was in the neighborhood and weeks turned into months of hanging out (sometimes pretty late), barbecuing, watching TV and playing cards, etc., etc., etc.

Weekend after weekend, I would have to take inventory, much like I did when I wiped out at the beach. Only this time, the cost was much greater: time away from my kids and money lent to him to prevent foreclosure on his home, with the promise of his many "close to being closed" big business deals on the table. By the time I woke up, I was $30,000 further in debt and the times my children needed me most were gone. I had done what my father had done to me. I was very embarrassed and did not know how to undo it all. I am still amazed I did not lose my business. Thank you, God, for being with me in the thick of it.

Lesson Number One: If pain is not dealt with completely and true healing attained, dating can be just as painful as the divorce.

Thank God I had someone I could go to that would listen, minister to me and get me back on track. Twenty-five years from when we met, I went and knocked on my youth minister's door. Only now, he was the owner of a marriage and family counseling center, an international business coach and ready to take a nap before going to job number two. He waved me in and proceeded to minister to me for two hours, sharing about God's grace and the importance of being in relationship with mature Christian friends.

I began attending the Vineyard Church in Rancho Santa Margarita. This was a very intimate church with one service of about a hundred in attendance. There, I began my journey on the road to greater intimacy with God. I received more of God's healing and began living more in the light and awareness of God's voice.

Lesson Number Two: A healthy relationship is born out of discernment rather than neediness.

After several months of crying at church, picking up the financial pieces and going through an intensive year-long twelve step program for co-dependency, I met a great guy. Actually, my youth minister introduced me to him. I was surprised to find myself attracted to a nice, kind of nerdy, guy for a change. He was a true man of God and courted me. He treated me as God intended His royal daughters to be treated. I gave my heart away early in the relationship because I knew that we had mutual friends that could speak to his character. However, God was not yet finished with me.

My finances were a mess. My children were crying out in pain. I was making a complete change in my social structure, from friends from the marriage to new friends from church. My prince in shining armor, sadly, was recovering from his own disappointment in a failed marriage. He was just discovering who he was after years of self-denial and doing all he could to make things work. He was kind and helpful to me. I began to rely on him for my spiritual growth and would later recognize I had made him an idol. As he began to pull away, my abandonment issues kicked in strong and I became clingy. On Christmas, he showered me with presents. The day after Christmas he let me know he did not see long-term prospects with our relationship. I was devastated. I did all I could to not throw up right then and there. By the grace of God, I was able to tell him that I would always appreciate that he treated me with honor and respect and taught me how my Father in heaven would want His daughter to be treated by a man. I felt that God had given me a great man and had taken him away because I began to idolize him.

Lesson Number Three: Only God can meet all of our needs and even good men are not perfect.

This is when God got a hold of me in a great way. I began a twenty-one day fast from sugar, meat, caffeine and bread (basically a diet of fruit, nuts and vegetables). I could not sleep at night and was tormented by lies from the enemy. Thoughts like, "You screwed up, you will always screw up, you will never be financially sound, you will never be married to a man like that," ran through my head. I journaled, prayed, listened to worship music and continued with recovery ministries at the church. I began to experience gifts of the Holy Spirit and began to run in groups that developed those gifts. As a part of recovery, one learns to give back. Being on a ministry team gave me the opportunity for further healing and to shift from self-pity to helping others.

I resolved not to get involved in any romantic relationships for a while and sought a deeper relationship with God. God, the creator of all things, also has a sense of humor. I was sitting at Starbuck's, engaged in my routine of journaling and reading the Bible, when this guy wearing bicycle gear walked in and pointed at me. "Cherie, right? I remember you. We met a few months ago at the Starbuck's down the road."

Several months previous, I had shared part of my journal with him about this great guy that God had brought into my life. I had encouraged him that God had someone for him. I had told him to just seek God first and God would bring him someone special too.

He asked if he could sit with me and I told him he could. Then he asked about my boyfriend and was pleased we were no longer dating.

After that day we met several times for coffee together. I enjoyed our conversations. He let me know that he was sad for me, but his heart leapt when I told him I no longer had a boyfriend. I was slow to give my phone number and eventually accepted a lunch invitation. He let me know that he was coming up on two years of sobriety. But, I knew God was a gracious God and this man deserved a chance. He sent me flowers, made me laugh and would quickly re-arrange his schedule to help me with a computer problem. He had owned a computer repair and informational technology business. He also helped me organize my finances into the computer program, Quicken, as he was a controller for his current company.

I thanked God that He had brought me someone to bring levity into my life and help me with those things in which I struggle. But, I had learned from my last boyfriend and other wise mentors that I needed to keep everything, including my relationships with men, in the light. I decided that the next time I was to meet with my ministry team leader I would tell him about my new friend.

When I did speak to my team leader, I was surprised by his reaction. "Cherie," he said. "I have seen this so many times! A woman is doing well and beginning to assume more responsibilities in the church and then the enemy brings a man in who knocks her off course. I have seen women actually leave the church because of this."

Wow! What a wakeup call! My new relationship had seemed like it was from God. I was laughing again and he was very helpful. But then I remembered some other things I had noticed about my new friend. One time when we were waiting in line at Subway I saw impatience that I had not seen up to that moment. The situation did not seem to warrant the reaction that took place.

My leader went on to say that it was critical that we just be friends while I continued to heal. The recent breakup had opened up some wounds that God wanted to heal. "He won't be able to heal you if you take a shortcut and just put on a Band-Aid™." I reflected on how much I wanted God's healing.

"Let's see what this guy does with this," my leader continued. "If he truly wants a healthy relationship then he will walk through this and give you time. I am happy to sit down with the two of you. If that were to happen, I would tell him to continue to work on his sobriety."

I did not want to jeopardize the work God has been doing in me and I could not do something that might harm my children further. They needed me to be healthy and right with God. So this time around I kept my heart guarded. I listened to my leader and decided to apply the brakes on this new relationship.

I wish I could stand here and say I was as eloquent and tidy as my leader had suggested, but it took some time to end the relationship. The guy seemed to be understanding and willing to do whatever it took, but he struggled with the boundaries I placed and took it personally. I tried not to give mixed messages but I did, as I enjoyed time with him and I greatly appreciated his help. But he wanted more than I was willing to give at the time. The more I tried to set boundaries the more rejection he experienced. It was far from a smooth development.

I learned a lot from this situation, though. This time I had been open with my friends and my church leaders about my new friend. I had kept things in the light and let God work it out. I had listened and acted on wise counsel as quickly as I could. As a result, neither my children nor I ended up in emotional trouble as we had earlier in my life when I acted out of my neediness and without Godly counsel.

Recently, a dear person in my life commented on the changes she has seen in me. "Cherie," she said. "You are no longer that rambunctious girl struggling against your Father, but you are resting into His arms. You are allowing Him to do the work He wants to do in you, so that He can bless you to be a blessing to others."

I agreed with her. I have finally learned to trust God's ways and to let Him protect me.

Oh and by the way, under the mutual commitment to God and the covering of a pastoral counselor, God did eventually give me a husband. My Starbucks man fought for me and he truly fits me like a glove. With God's leading we are fighting for the lives God intends for our family and those around us.

Adrian

While praying about where to start my journey, it came to me to start at the beginning. My heart's desire is for others to identify with part of my story and be comforted and encouraged.

For me it began in 1954. I was the first of two daughters. The fifties and early sixties were a wonderful time to be a child. We lived in a model city, were raised in church and never worried about our parents getting divorced.

I always felt my mother did not understand me, like I was an alien, except for the fact I looked just like my dad. Mom and I were always like night and day. I was an anxious child from an early age. As soon as I was able to sit up, I began to bounce, much to my mother's horror. In any place that had a soft back, I would throw myself forward and then back, bouncing my head off the seat. I can still remember feeling the release of tension with every bounce. It was good therapy! At age four, my parents finally broke me of this habit.

Although in most ways it was an ideal life, there was always tension between my mom and me. I often felt she was unhappy with me. I climbed trees and was very proud of my skill. I enlisted the neighbor kids in my own version of boot camp. I had them climbing trees, running around the block and walking the tops of our cinder block fences. But, Mom wanted a little girl to dress up in frills.

I loved elementary school. I did fair with my studies, but was a goddess on the playground. I performed death-defying acts on the bars and ruled hopscotch. In the sixth grade, I was the fastest runner in my school. I competed in district track meets and loved every minute of it.

As I entered junior high, I had an identity crisis. What, no playground? My anxiety flared, which kicked me into a state of ADD. All those classrooms, books, lockers and ninth graders! I felt there was no place for me there. My grades tanked, I was miserable and confused and had nowhere to shine.

It was the time of big hair and short skirts. So, I became known for my short skirts and big hair. I was still quite innocent at the time, but I was attracting the wrong kind of people.

Sometime in the eighth grade I was introduced to drugs. I was such a ripe candidate. My first experience was with pills. It was like being back on the couch, bouncing. I escaped from my anxiety. I had no idea this was the beginning of a pattern that would follow me for much of my life. Later it was marijuana; in my mind it cured broken hearts, boredom and anything else that ailed me.

As kids, we attended a small church; it was wonderful. I think we were there every time they opened the doors. My parents served and all of their best friends were there. I believe I was around eleven when we had a rift at our little church. We were among those that left. We started attending regularly at what would be a mega-church in those days. I never connected there. By the time junior high came around, I wanted nothing to do with the junior high group; I did not fit in. I was the one with a snarly look on my face that said I am only here because my parents made me.

I grew up in church and I did know for sure Jesus loved me and I loved Him, but I was too immature to know that Jesus was also the answer to what was missing in my life.

By the time I entered high school, drugs were a big part of my life. School was where I went to see my friends and get around any rule I could. Somehow I did manage to graduate. At twenty-four, I married my high school sweetheart. Drugs were still a part of my recreation and even became what I turned to at home on a lonely night, a sad night or to perk me up.

When I was twenty-six years old, Jesus came down and flooded me with love. I had a co-worker who I knew was praying for me, but I was not giving God the time of day, until through some of my own bad choices, I was fired from my job that I loved. That same night, as I lay crying in my bed, the Lord comforted me in a very tangible way. I felt warmth as though I was being wrapped in love and grace. First

John 4:19 tells us that we love because He first loved us. God used this opportunity of feeling loved to draw me to Him.

It was at that time that I also fell in love with God through His Word, the Bible, and by His Spirit. I was moving on from my Sunday school relationship with the Lord. I felt loved and accepted just the way I was.

Over time, God changed the desires of my heart. I began to live out the truth of Psalm 37:4, "Delight yourself in the Lord and he will give you the desires of your heart."

During this time I was trying to get pregnant. I pleaded with the Lord for a child. After a long five years, we had our baby. We named him Samuel, which means, "asked of God." Oh what a celebration! He was the first grandchild, prayed for by many over the years. Now I really thought I had found my calling: to be a mother. He was a delight! I became the mom that made sure everything that went into his mouth was nutritious and no television! I was a very devoted mother.

When Sam was four his father left me and I fell apart. Life changed so dramatically for Sam and me; I couldn't stop crying and was not very functional. Suddenly the television was my babysitter. My heart broke for myself and for my son.

I began trying to make up for the fact that Sam's dad had left. I set about to make him happy, wanting nothing to ever hurt him again.

As I write this, my four-year-old grandson is in the other room waiting for the call that his cousins are home so he can go over to play. As he waits, I get anxious that it will get too late and he won't get to play. All I can think of is how I can make him happy so he doesn't have to experience disappointment. Those were the same misguided feelings I'd had and acted on with Sam.

I sincerely believed God would restore my marriage; He hates divorce, right? But He didn't and in my grief I became angry with God. I pushed Him out and once again began my own pain management.

After several months of sitting home alone, I felt I needed some relief. I wasn't plugged in with any Christian friends at the time. A co-worker invited me to the Crazy Horse Saloon. I thought, "What the heck, I like country music. Sounds like fun." As a young adult I had spent a lot of time in bars so I felt right at home. Before I knew it, the Crazy Horse was my new hang out. I shared many a tear in my beer with the other recently divorced lonely hearts.

As always, the Lord had my back. I was thirty-five going on twenty-one again. I had crushes on lots of cute cowboys, but the Lord closed doors on all but one, my Brian. After several years of on and off dating, we married.

We continued to frequent the Crazy Horse, until one day when the Lord came down and flooded Brian with love. That's another story, but a good one, so I'll tell you.

We were at my ninety-year-old grandmother's funeral. She was a strong Christian woman. Near the end of her memorial service, the pastor invited anyone who did not know the Lord to say a prayer with him to invite Jesus into his or her life and to accept the gift of forgiveness for his or her sins. Brian may have been the only person there who did not know the Lord. At one point, I looked over at him and he was crying, I mean really crying. I thought it was odd since he wasn't close with my grandma. Right there, in Corona, California, the Lord gave Brian eyes to see and ears to hear. Brian had a Saul of Tarsus conversion: everything changed in a heartbeat. We began attending church and the Crazy Horse began to fade away.

Sometime around the age of twelve, Sam began experimenting with drugs, possibly for the same reasons I did: anxiety and escape. So began the heartache of my beloved Samuel. Over the years to come, the life Brian and I shared became consumed with getting help for Sam. I took Sam to all the leading therapists and psychiatrists. He would go to appointments on drugs and con the therapist. The spiritual battle was tangible in Sam and in our home. One day, I called a fellow challenged parent and told her, "I smell hell." Turns out I forgot to turn my iron off!

One night when Sam was sixteen he was angry with Brian for drug testing him. He called his dad to come and get him and he never came home to live with us again. What a blow! Before, we had been on top of everywhere he went. Now, Sam had a new found freedom. His drug use quickly spiraled out of control.

Then there was my motherhood. I loved being Sam's mom; parenting was what I was supposed to excel at! Up to this point I hadn't been very sympathetic to women whose children weren't living with them; I was maybe even judgmental. Since then, my heart aches for women who don't have their children with them for any reason. My own heart certainly broke over Sam's departure. I knew there would be no high school graduation or any of the other milestones that you and your child celebrate as they ease into leaving home. By age seventeen Sam was a full-blown drug addict.

I finally figured out I was the one that needed guidance; Sam wasn't ready. The best decision I made was to find a counselor for myself. Parenting a drug addict is not in the parenting manuals. Exercising tough love often goes against all motherly instincts. Often times, following my mother's heart was enabling Sam. My counselor helped guide me through the troubled waters.

By this time, we were meeting weekly with families of children who were struggling with an assortment of issues. The first time we met, I began to cry, finally being in a group of people who really "got it."

Our parent group became a tightly knit little family. We shared our pain, anger and even despair at times. We laughed together, too. Of course, you have to keep your sense of humor. And we prayed!

Although God didn't always answer our prayers in our timing, we did see countless miracles. One of our moms had a daughter who had run away to Utah. That was all the information she had. It was near Mother's Day and she was aching to see her girl. The plan was for her to fly to Utah and hope for the best. Our prayer was that she would find her daughter quickly so she would at least have some time to spend with her. When our mom landed in Utah her daughter was waiting for her at the airport. She had called home to wish her mother "Happy Mother's Day" and her dad told her of the plan!

Sam is a handsome man and has good manners so he was able to couch surf in our city for many years. But, I would not hear from him for weeks or months at a time. Not knowing if your child is dead or alive is a dreadful way to live. I had connections in Yorba Linda that would confirm he was still alive. Every time I left my house I looked at the young men walking by to see if one of them might be Sam. Then there were mothers and sons at the grocery store that would remind me of his younger years. Inevitably I would go home and cry my eyes out.

One night I thought my heart would burst if I did not lay eyes on my son. I heard he was staying at a hotel in town. I walked the corridors of the hotel calling his name. It only made me feel more helpless. I was studying Hosea and came across a passage titled "God's love for Israel." I cried when I learned God knew exactly what I was feeling as a parent. Hosea 11 is all about God's love for Israel, His children. I really saw God's heart in verses three and four. The Lord says, "It was I who taught Ephraim to walk, taking them by the arms; but they did not realize it was I who healed them. I led them with cords of human kindness, with ties of love; I lifted the yoke from their neck and bent down to feed them." Indeed, the Lord knows the broken heart of a parent. As a parent, I felt the need to be doing something, anything, to help my wounded child.

One summer, as I sought the Lord daily for guidance, He gave me this verse from Psalm 27:14, "Wait for the LORD; be strong and take heart and wait for the LORD." I was amazed at how many different ways God could tell me to "wait on Him and do nothing." When our children are hurting, it is difficult to do nothing. Sam was in his twenties by then; it was time to hand him over to the Lord. Sam was aware of God at a very young age and as a young teen, he accepted Christ as his Savior. He once had a deep relationship with God, but it seemed short lived.

During this time, Brian and I learned what praying in earnest meant. It was such a crazy way to live. Brian and I had a good life, but I always had a dark cloud over my head, a pain in my heart. I lived what I called the "express life," which looked like, "Yes, I'll make it to the family event, but don't expect me to bring anything. It's all I can do to get there." It wasn't that I did not receive from the Lord; I lived off His promises, but I was grieving what felt like unending loss.

It was the best of times and the worst of times. We bought our modest dream home with a pool in the back yard. I poured myself into the house; every square foot had our mark on it. We had countless Bible studies in our home and made so many new friends. We shared openly about our trials, which allowed others to do the same. God was also blessing Brian's kitchen and bath remodeling company. He considered it not only a business, but also a ministry. Over the years, many came to know Christ through the business.

Then things changed.

On Monday morning, October 27, 2007, my phone rang at around 6:00 a.m. My first thought was fear. I had received many late night/early morning phone calls concerning Sam. It ran through my mind that this could be the call that I'd lived in dread of; "Your son Samuel is dead." The woman on the phone told me, "Your husband has been in a car accident and we think he may have had a stroke."

I went into my survival mode. I drove to the hospital.

Apparently, I had called some friends before I left. I only know this because some of them beat me to the emergency room. Brian had temporarily lost his sight during the stroke. He'd been on his way to work on a busy street, when he went off road through an orange grove and landed in a culvert. He didn't have a scratch on him. I have walked the site and it is hard to believe how he sailed through that grove without hitting a tree, one of the many miracles to come.

When I got to Brian, the stroke seemed mild. The doctor and I went back and forth whether to administer the TPA shot also known as the clot buster. It was finally decided the risk was too high. As the hours went by, Brian's stroke turned into a bleed in his brain. It soon became apparent this was a life-threatening situation.

Brian got sicker by the day. He had lost function in the right side of his brain and was completely paralyzed on his left side. Here was a man who had been surfing the day before his stroke and now he was never to work again, drive, or enjoy many of the activities he had before, nor many we as a couple had enjoyed!

By days five and six, Brian was in and out of consciousness. My friend Denise and I were in his room along with a nurse. His vitals were at dangerous levels and he was not responding to me. Eventually he opened his eyes and said, "There is a battle going on for my life." Knowing he had committed the fifth chapter of Ephesians to memory, I asked him to tell me about the "full armor of God." As he recited this passage, his blood pressure came down and he became more aware of his surroundings. It was a turning point in his recovery. The three of us in that room knew we had witnessed something miraculous. The power of God's Word defeated Satan.

Brian left the hospital and went to a rehabilitation facility, where he began his fight for recovery: learning to sit, walk and care for himself again. After fifty-three days, Brian returned home. It was still the beginning of his journey; he was weak, but it was not in his personality or in his faith to give up. He is my wounded warrior.

This would be a good time to share with you the support and love we have experienced from the body of Christ. Brian had rehabilitation appointments several times a week, so someone at our church organized rides for him. So many people wanted to help, there actually became a waiting list to give Brian rides. At first, it was very difficult to ask or receive help. My first move was to accept a neighbor's offer to walk our dog; you would have thought I was the one giving her a blessing! When Brian came home from the hospital, our friends arranged for us to have meals every night for many months. The prayers and outpouring of love was overwhelming. Many lasting friendships were built during that time.

The first year, Brian's loyal employees and I tried to keep his business going. Brian had been the financial manager in our relationship, but now he wasn't making any decisions. After putting all of our resources into the business, we finally had to say goodbye to it. Closing the business was physically, mentally and emotionally difficult. I really didn't know where to start. A man at our church had heard of our situation and called me. He said he had his own business and that he thought about what it would be like if his wife were in my position. Mind you, I had never met this man before. He took complete charge of the physical closing of the business. He and many men from church and employees dismantled the large show room and warehouse, selling all of it. What could have been a devastating time turned into a blessing, because of all the love that was poured out on us.

Once my time was no longer consumed with the business, I had to face the future. I had been living in denial that our situation was as dire as it was. I really believed God would intervene somehow in our finances. Reality was that it was time to sell our home, which meant we would be moving in with my parents. I loved our home and wanted to pass it off at its best. All those little things I had still wanted to do I completed. It took several months to sell. Meantime, my sister Kelly and I began downsizing and packing. Kelly was a storm trooper, the sergeant of the move. We were so organized; Emily Barnes would have been impressed. We had an estate sale, where everything was displayed as if it was an actual store. I was not parting with my treasures at a yard sale! Very little was left and the rest I put in storage or took to my parents. At the end of the day, I felt grateful to God for my family and friends.

Once moved into my parents' home, it all began to sink in. I grew up with a loving, caring and protective father, whom I respected very much. My image of God the Father was greatly influenced by my relationship with my dad. My earthly father would not have allowed me to suffer such loss if it were in his power to change it. I was now learning that our Heavenly Father is concerned with much more than our creature comfort. As it says in James 1:2-4, "Consider it pure joy, my brothers, whenever you face trials of many kinds, because you know that the testing of your faith develops perseverance. Perseverance must finish its work so that you may be mature and complete, not lacking anything. "

God was blowing the box I had put Him in to smithereens.

Part of my role at my parents' home was care-giving for my mother and my husband, although I felt like I had nothing to give. I was now living so many situations of which I had said, "I could never . . . ."

Instead of accepting my situation, I began to unravel spiritually, mentally and physically. I was so hard on myself. I wanted to glorify God. I wanted to react as Paul and Silas did after being stripped, beaten and severely flogged. They were put in jail with their feet in iron stocks. Then, around midnight, people heard them praying to God and singing hymns. When thinking of Paul's life, I have to remember it was a process to learn the secret of being content in any and every circumstance. I imagine he learned from the many trials he suffered as he saw the power of God in his life. Paul could do all things through Christ who gave him strength. I had yet to learn how. I was and still am, a work in progress.

At my parent's home, my depression and anxiety rose. I began the grief process. In the beginning, one of my heartaches was the loss of our home. I no longer had a "home of my own." I missed my fireplace, my bathroom that I had designed myself, the privacy and the pool, where we had loved entertaining. I missed the peace and quiet.

After much time had gone by, I cried out to God, "What do I do with these memories of my home? How can I move on?"

Then something unusual happened. Since I am a very visual person, it was as if the Lord took me on a visual healing tour. In my mind, Jesus and I went to my home and we walked every square foot together. We went room to room saying goodbye to my treasured things and moments in time. One at a time, I wrapped each room and handed it to Jesus and closed the door. I asked Jesus to put those memories in a safe place for me. I had been carrying them around on my back way too long and it was crushing me.

Next, the Lord and I had to address the fact that I was angry that we had no money. We were now living on Brian's social security check. Once again I was humbled. As much as I hate to admit it, there was a time that I had looked at people in our situation and thought, "No one can have that much bad luck and they must be doing something wrong." Fortunately, we did not have friends like Job, who had to beg his friends to believe he hadn't brought his troubles onto himself.

God had released me from these past hurts; I now needed healing for the present and the future. My head filled with thoughts like, "How would we ever buy a new car? What will happen to us when my parents pass away? Will we be homeless?" How scary at our age not to have any plan for the future, especially when previously we thought we had it all figured out.

God does faithfully provide us with manna, or provisions for the day, but like the Israelites in the Bible did, I grumbled and complained at times. I preferred a warehouse of manna, not just a day's supply. Like the Israelites, I was unhappy with the Lord's provisions.

In my mind, relief could only come if my circumstances changed. Well, they did not, no matter how many times I entered the Publishers Clearing House Sweepstakes.

By this time, Sam had completed a year and a half in Teen Challenge, a faith based recovery program. He married a wonderful woman and they had a son who is the light of my life. For the first six months I was at my parents' house, I poured myself into our grandson. He was a year and a half old at the time. I would pick him up nearly every day and off we would go. You could often see us at the park or some random Little League game. "Love Bug" would help me with the laundry, tossing items in the washer one piece at a time with a huff and a puff. Then, for the finale, I would let him push the buttons to start the washer. The bath was his favorite place to be, so I always gave him a bath. We loved to walk after dark so he could run up all the driveways and set off the motion sensor lights. We looked for stars and checked out the moon. He made me very happy. Of course, I loved his parents, too.

Right after Bug's second birthday, he and his parents abruptly moved to Washington State. There went all my kiddies! My sister refers to this time as when my wheels began to fall off. I became increasingly depressed, irritable and tired. I never felt good, sometimes not too bad, but never good. I missed church, parties and many other events. At times, I didn't even feel well enough to shower and get dressed. This state of not feeling well I call the "cruds." It felt kind of like I was wearing a couple of those vests they give you when you're getting an x-ray. My chest felt heavy. At times, I had a screaming headache for weeks. Once, our friends treated us to an amazing hotel that overlooked the ocean and I spent the entire day in bed looking out the window.

I started taking a pain pill in the afternoon, which seemed to clear up my cruds for a couple of hours. This got me through chores or getting ready to go somewhere. I began to look forward to that late afternoon pain pill, whether I really needed it or not. It became an escape.

At the time, the only thing the doctors could diagnose was depression. I found out later there were also medical issues too. Previously, I had not fully understood how someone could be debilitated by depression. Now I get it and once again, I've been humbled.

When my kids would call, I had absolutely nothing new to say to them. I felt like the walking dead. The confident woman I had become was nowhere to be seen. I allowed my mother to take our relationship back to when I was fifteen. I was becoming the insecure, not very bright, never measuring up, always in trouble, teenager. Caring for my mother as she became bedridden and increasingly difficult was crushing me. Those near to me were becoming very concerned. They did all they could to cheer me. I do have the best friends ever and Brian was so patient with me, but evening after evening I would melt down. The only answer he had was to trust the Lord. Brian had never-ending grace for me. I am so ashamed to admit that he often got the brunt of my frustration.

I knew in my head that God would never leave me and I also knew that God uses all things for the good of those who love Him and are called according to His purposes. Oh yes, I believed all those things were true. And from the book of James I remembered to "count it all joy," and that trials test our faith. I decided if I was being tested that I had failed with a big, fat F. I thought, "If this is a test, Lord, you might have thought about ending it somewhere between 'I can't breathe' and 'maybe You could just give me a heart attack.'" No disrespect was meant to the Lord. I had no peace, no joy and the worst of all, no hope.

I grieved quietly and not so quietly into my pillow. I considered tearing my clothes like the ancient Jews did, thinking it might help, but I didn't want to scare the family.

I wrote a note on a piece of paper that said, "We are in a war; the battle is not mine. I feel as though I have had a sword run through me and I need to go to the infirmary. Lord, what does that look like? Please help me. Putting on my armor, abiding—all those verbs seem so daunting to me. Lord, pull me out of the mire. I am road kill; road kill cannot receive anything."

I tucked the piece of paper away and forgot about it. About two weeks later, the Lord sent a faithful friend to the rescue. She said she was going to an individual retreat center and asked if I wanted to go, too. I spent two amazing nights there. It was a beautiful Spanish style mansion, built in the 1920's and nestled in the hills of Montecito. It sits on acres and acres. I was in awe of the peace and quiet. You had to whisper in the house and even wear slippers so your shoes wouldn't make any noise. A big part of my anxiety comes from noise. I live in a house with three very hard of hearing people who watch television day and night.

I prepared to hear from the Lord with my Bible, pad and pencil in hand. Oh my sweet Lord, He knows road kill cannot concentrate. Instead, He ministered to my soul. I had my own beautiful little room. There were French doors next to my bed and large windows overlooking the lush, green hills. I love to soak in a tub and my room had an oversized bathtub that I soaked in every chance I got. What a blessing! Dinner was served family style at an antique dining table. It was so relaxing, chatting with the other guests, sharing the various circumstances that brought each of us to this place. On the grounds there are many little gardens to sit and mediate in. There is also a labyrinth made of rocks. This was new to me. You were supposed to walk this maze and connect with God. Several people asked me if I had walked the labyrinth. I thought, "It's just a bunch of rocks. No, I think I will pass." On the last afternoon another guest told me I should walk the labyrinth, so I thought, "Why not?"

I began my walk prayerfully. With each leg of the walk I felt God revealing truths to me. It was my spiritual journey, where He and I had been together. I was overwhelmed with gratefulness. We looked at the sorrows and the joys. I was reminded He had been with me every step of the way. The last leg was very short and I felt the Lord saying to me that it wouldn't always be this way. It had been too long since I had received from the Lord like this. Most importantly, He gave me hope.

At home, I later found the note I had written crying out for God to rescue me. When I had written that note, I hadn't known He already had a plan to send me to the "infirmary" and to restore my soul. So, on the same piece of paper, I recorded Psalm 40:1-2, "I waited patiently for the LORD; he turned to me and heard my cry. He lifted me out of the slimy pit, out of the mud and mire; he set my feet on a rock and gave me a firm place to stand. He put a new song in my mouth, a hymn of praise to our God."

I wish I could say the battle was over. Slowly, I took my eyes off the Lord and turned back to focusing on my circumstances. Like Peter, I began to sink. I etched out an existence for myself to survive. Whenever possible, I slept until noon and stayed up until two or three in the morning. Having the house to myself late at night was just too good. I beat myself up for having such an unacceptable lifestyle.

I remember telling my dad one Sunday night that something had to give. The next morning I woke up around seven. I lay in my bed thinking *I can't do this for one more day*. I just kept repeating, "Help me Jesus." I felt so trapped; I had to get out. I have a friend who lives in Laguna Beach. She often told me that I could stay in her guesthouse anytime. It was a divine appointment. I called and explained my situation and asked if I could come for two nights. Oh and one more thing. I asked her, "Can you pick me up as I don't think I can drive."

I felt as though I was running away from home, which I had never done before. I lined up caregivers for my parents and Ana picked me up by noon. She was not going to let me sleep for two days. Monday night we went to a church service. I remember trying to worship. I was sitting with my face in my hands. The pastor came over and spoke a few words over me. What caught my attention was that he said he could see something like a beehive buzzing around my head.

Later, when I was alone in the quiet guest room, I closed my eyes and listened. The pastor was right on. As I sat in silence, I focused on what was going on in my head. It was like a beehive humming in my head. It's called anxiety. I could not distinguish between what was my own negative voice, the enemy's, or the Lord's. It was frightening; no wonder I was worn out. I prayed and asked the Lord to take it away.

I woke up in the middle of the night to silence. My mind was calm; it felt so different. Then it dawned on me: *this is what peace feels like*. To this day, I have not experienced that kind of chaos in my head again. It felt like spring in my head and heart. Now when I have a negative thought, I say, "That is not from you Jesus."

After coming home from my respite, I felt so functional. I knew I had been minimizing and rationalizing my self-medicating. Once I admitted that to myself, I went to a meeting called *Celebrate Recovery*—a Christian twelve-step program. What I didn't expect was to hear myself, on the stage with a microphone, admitting I had a problem with prescription drugs. When I got home that night, with the covers pulled up over my head, I thought, "Say it isn't so!" I thought I would go back the next week and explain to them that I had just gotten caught up in the moment. I felt as though I'd let a genie out of a bottle and I wanted it back in!

I so desperately wanted to stop taking that late afternoon pill that I had come to depend on. It wasn't working anymore. I felt like a prisoner. I went back to *Celebrate Recovery* as often as I could and I liked it. I got over my pride and once again was humbled.

Today, I want the Lord to use all my experiences for good. I know there are others like me. I want them to know they are not alone with their weaknesses, their guilt and their shame.

Today I ask myself, "*Did Jesus conquer the power of sin and death at the cross, or not? Can I do all things through Christ who gives me strength?*" He is showing me I can!

Through every trial of my life, I come away with new tools, new wisdom for living in the day. And that is why I now can say Philippians 4:4-7.

> *Rejoice in the Lord always. I will say it again: Rejoice! Let your gentleness be evident to all. The Lord is near. Do not be anxious about anything, but in everything, by prayer and petition, with thanksgiving, present your requests to God. And the peace of God, which transcends all understanding, will guard your hearts and your minds in Christ Jesus.*

Tami

You keep him in perfect peace whose mind is stayed on you, because he trusts in you. Isaiah 26:3 (ESV)

Before I can share a most difficult six-year period of my life and be open and honest, revealing to you my deepest struggles, fears and pain, I must give you a brief look into the fabric of my life. In reading this, perhaps you will see yourself in some of my experiences and be encouraged.

I grew up in a home where there was little love shown between my parents. The mood was always tense, as I had a strict disciplinarian and perfectionist for a father and an emotionally distant mother. They always seemed to be at odds with each other. As hard as my brothers and I tried, it seemed nothing we ever did was good enough to meet Dad's approval. The mental and emotional abuse I suffered as a child still holds a significant grip on who I am today.

As I was growing up, my father pastored many churches and my view of God was greatly skewed, because what he preached on Sunday wasn't what we lived at home. I always say, "We lived like heaven on Sundays and like hell the rest of the week." In my teens and upward I witnessed both my parents' infidelity and their divorce. My father left the pastorate, remarried twice and lived with other women several times. My innocence as a young teen was lost through a dark period of molestation by a family friend. I experienced fear and anger at my father's multiple suicide attempts. My husband and I had many heartbreaking years dealing with my infertility issues and then the loss of our first three babies through miscarriage. There was also the loss of my mother to brain cancer and the twenty-plus years of physical pain because of fibromyalgia and other health issues.

As I look back over my life and the many difficult experiences I've had, experiences probably not much different than some of yours, I can now see God's hand covering them all. As I journeyed through these things, however, I didn't always sense God's presence and many times wondered where He was and why He didn't make these things stop. I often questioned my own faith. But as I now look back, I can see His arms were always around me even though I didn't always believe it; that He never let go of me and that He was gently teaching me to trust and know that *"He is the LORD my God, who upholds my right hand, who says to me, 'do not fear, I will help you.'"*

It was Monday morning May 7, 2007 and I was excitedly looking forward to Saturday when my husband, Everett and I would be leaving for a belated thirty-fifth wedding anniversary trip to Hawaii. Our older son, Keith, had just married two months previously and I was still high on the memories of that beautiful day when our lovely daughter-in-law, Kim, joined the family.

Just before 9:00 a.m. as I was heading out the door for a routine doctor visit, the phone rang. Sarah, my other daughter-in-law, was on the other end of the phone and I couldn't believe what she was saying. Our younger son, Kevin, had fallen off a ladder at work and was taken unconscious to the hospital. My mind was racing, *"What did she say? This isn't real. How bad is he? He's unconscious? That can't be good. Will he die before we can get to him?"* I told Sarah to hold on while I called Everett so we could all drive to the hospital together.

"You will keep him in perfect peace whose mind is stayed on you..."

As we drove to the hospital, which was a good hour away, Sarah received another call from Kevin's supervisor who said Kevin was in a coma, but other details were sketchy at best. I began calling several of my closest friends and frantically asked them to start praying that Kevin would be okay.

"You will keep him in perfect peace whose mind is stayed on you..."

There it was again, part of a verse I had learned long ago but couldn't remember the rest of. It didn't matter. I knew God had spoken those words to me, words that would reverberate through my mind for months to come. As we drove, I pleaded with God, begging Him to protect Kevin and to give him back to us whole.

Once we reached the hospital, we were ushered into a waiting room, where Kevin's supervisor met us. He was visibly shaken, which didn't do anything to reduce my fears. We all huddled together and prayed, asking God to take care of Kevin.

After what seemed an eternity, Kevin's trauma doctor came in to see us. I couldn't comprehend all she was saying, but what I did understand wasn't good. Kevin's skull was fractured in two places; he had come to the hospital in a coma and was going to be kept in a medically induced coma because there was bleeding and swelling of the brain. A neurosurgeon was being called in.

When I was first allowed into the ICU, I couldn't take in all I was seeing. Kevin was hooked up to several monitors, with so many tubes leading to his body that I couldn't count them all. There was a tube down his throat, he was wearing a cervical collar and was breathing with the aid of a ventilator. An eerie-looking metal tube was protruding from his skull, monitoring swelling in his brain. I felt I would faint and life suddenly became surreal.

Kevin had suffered a traumatic brain injury; he laid in a coma for six agonizing weeks and each day there was the real threat that he wouldn't make it to the next. Those weeks were six of the hardest and most painful of my life. And, this was only the beginning of six trying years, years that tested my faith and shook me to the very core of my being, but brought me to the feet of Jesus. But at this moment I was asking, *"Where is that perfect peace God had promised?"*

I cannot begin to express the deep pain in my heart and the sheer helplessness of a mother unable to help her son. We were at the mercy of doctors, surgeons and nurses. But above all, I knew Kevin's life was dependent upon the mercy of God.

I was unable to sleep the third night after Kevin's accident and my heart was breaking, as I didn't know whether he would make it through another night. My mind wandered back to many moments of Kevin as he was growing up. As tears rolled down my cheeks, I remembered something I had always told the boys when they were old enough to go somewhere away from my supervision, desiring their best behavior. As they would head out the door, I would point up to the sky and say, "Just remember whose son you are." That night, I cried out to God about the agony of watching my son suffer so. He gently spoke to me and told me He understood exactly what I was feeling as He too had watched His son suffer horribly and that no matter what happened to Kevin, He would be right there to hold me up. As I cried even more, I realized anew that Kevin was not just my son, but was also a son of God. And if God chose to take him home, everything would be alright, because Kevin would be forever with the Lord he loved.

Six weeks is a long time to hold your breath, but that is what it felt I was doing. Kevin's life was in such a precarious condition that we knew we could lose him at any moment. We spent interminable hours waiting for the results of tests and procedures, waiting for any piece of good news. I kept praying that the swelling in his brain would stop, willing him to breathe on his own, to open his eyes and speak. Each day blurred into the next.

I was too numb to pray and couldn't understand why this had happened. This sort of thing only happens to other people. Suddenly, I realized I was "other people." *"Oh God, I have endured so much pain in my life already. Why do I have to endure this as well? This just hurts too much. What are you trying to teach me?"* I cried this over and over in my heart.

I have always struggled with intimacy with God. I asked Jesus into my heart when I was only six, but as a child I couldn't fully comprehend what having a relationship with Jesus really meant.

The hypocrisy of my upbringing only served to mar my image of God. At the age of fifteen, when I was being molested and had pleaded with God to not let it happen again, only to have it happen time after time, I was only distanced further from God. At that same time, the relationship between my parents was at an all-time low. My mother was having an affair with a man in the church; my dad was having one of his mysterious "illnesses" and attempted suicide. Things at the church where he pastored were volatile to say the least. The fighting and arguing between them was so bad that I hated being at home. I was jealous of my older brother who had joined the Marines as his way of escape. I felt trapped, alone. There was no one to turn to. I fought hard not to believe in God at all and for years there was a war raging in my heart. He always seemed so far away, but yet, so very near.

I had learned well how to play the part of a Christian. I was the good little preacher's kid and went to church three times a week with a smile on my face. As an adult, I served on committees, taught Sunday school, sang in the choir, worked as the church secretary and countless other things. On the outside I looked like the perfect Christian, but only God and I knew the struggle going on inside.

How eternally grateful I am that He had a firm grip on my life and He wasn't about to let me slip away. He had much to teach me to bring me fully to Him.

One day, in the first weeks following Kevin's accident, Kim and I were taking a break outside the waiting room. I tearfully shared with her how I believed God had been preparing me for this event. There have only been a couple instances in my life where I can say with conviction that God was speaking directly to me and this is one of them. I shared with Kim how several weeks before, as I would be praying during my daily time with the Lord, I could clearly hear Him say, "Pray for Kevin," and then I would hear, "You will be taking care of Sarah." This hadn't happened just once, but many times in those weeks before it came true.

Kevin had just started a new job as an industrial plumber a couple of months earlier. He had been employed in several jobs previously where I knew he could be in some physical danger, but I had never really given it much thought. My boys had always been in my prayers, but this was different. I began praying for Kevin in earnest. The thoughts of harm coming to him plagued my imagination. I couldn't understand what God was trying to say to me and I must admit I thought all of this had just been a figment of my vivid imagination, so I kept it to myself until that day. As I thought back through this once Kevin was home, I wondered how differently things might have turned out had I not heeded God's voice and prayed.

A couple of weeks into Kevin's hospitalization, my son, Keith and his new bride, Kim, were at our house doing laundry, because the washer at their house was broken. Kim called me at the hospital distressed because she had to tell me something terrible she had done. I couldn't imagine this precious girl doing anything so wrong that would have her so upset. She proceeded to tell me that she and Keith had had an argument and she had thrown a bowl of chocolate ice cream all over my carpet. The picture in my head was so comical that I burst out laughing. She couldn't believe I was taking it so well so I said to her, "Kim, in light of everything going on here, I can handle a little chocolate ice cream on my carpet."

God brought me back to that "chocolate-on-the-carpet" moment many times over the following months and years as I realized things that once seemed so important just didn't compare to almost losing a son. And because of the glory of heaven waiting for me, all the trials I face now are not worth the effort of getting upset. Maybe, just maybe, I was beginning to allow God to show me His perfect peace.

Around the fifth week, the doctors were able to start bringing Kevin out of the medically induced coma, because the pressure in his brain had finally subsided. Coming out of a coma is nothing like the Hollywood version, where the patient wakes up all smiles, ready to jump out of bed and get on with life. No, having a traumatic brain injury only makes the waking up period worse.   Kevin had to be put in restraints while coming out of the coma because he was becoming more and more aggressive. We were told this is typical of brain injury. No one can be prepared for the horror of it. We had no idea whether Kevin recognized any of us. He fought with and cursed at the nurses, therapists and just about anyone who came near him. *"God, is this what life is going to be like from now on? How will our family be able to cope with this? Will Kevin ever be himself again?"*

After the sixth week, Kevin was moved to a sub-acute rehabilitation center to grow physically strong enough to go to an acute rehabilitation center. The nightmare continued. As he "woke up" more and more from the coma and came out from under the influence of so many drugs, we got a better picture of what we were dealing with—and it was not pretty. He was also more and more aggressive, usually quite non-compliant with his therapists, doctors, nurses and family. My son, who had never cursed before, was cursing and screaming like a drunken sailor. His aggression lashed out at me and Sarah more than once. We both received punches from him. Once, Sarah found his hands around her throat trying to choke her.

I was physically, emotionally and spiritually exhausted. All the stress was causing my fibromyalgia to go on a rampage and there were days I didn't think I could take another step. There was no relief in sight and I was still not experiencing that perfect peace; where was the joy I, as a Christian, should be experiencing? Oh it was there, deep down somewhere in my heart, because I knew God was in control of the situation and that He could be trusted, but at that moment it just wasn't surfacing in my heart. I desperately wanted the past couple of months erased and my old son back.

The medical center was only a couple of miles from our home and I could go and visit Kevin every day. I would often sit and read the Scriptures to him. The book of Philippians was his favorite so I read that quite often. As I read, I wondered if this accident would cause him to lose his faith in God and become embittered towards Him. Most of the time I didn't think Kevin could hear me, but while I was reading, hoping to encourage him, I knew it was I who needed the encouragement.

God brought some of that much needed encouragement one afternoon when a close friend of Kevin's came to visit him. Kevin was having a particularly bad day and we had gotten him into a wheelchair to get him out of his room for a change of scenery. He was in a very foul mood, screaming and cursing at everyone to leave him alone as we wheeled him through the halls of the hospital. At one point his friend stooped down and began to talk to him very calmly. Kevin began to respond and the tantrum eased. His friend then asked him, "Kevin, do you know who Jesus is?" I can still hear him answer without hesitation, "He's my Lord and Savior." An enormous wave of relief washed over me. Even with his scrambled brain, I knew Kevin was trusting God.

After five weeks in the sub-acute rehabilitation center, skeleton thin and barely eating, Kevin was finally deemed physically well enough to be transferred to the Centre for Neuro Skills, an acute rehabilitation center in Bakersfield, California, a good two-hour drive from our home.

The morning arrived for him to be transferred. Sarah and I looked at each other in dismay as two young women came to pick him up; we were sure it would take a couple of burly men to handle him. It literally took us two hours to get him from his bed to the van as he fought all the way, even lying down in the middle of the hospital hallway refusing to get up. That fight continued the full two-hour drive to Bakersfield as Kevin tried forcing his way out of the van. He beat, scratched and bruised the young woman who sat next to him in the back of the van, trying to control him, as Sarah sat helplessly in the front seat next to the driver.

This behavior continued on through the night and the next day. That first full day at the Centre was traumatic for all of us. Sarah, Everett and I were allowed to follow Kevin around as the staff worked with him, showing us what the structure of his life would be for an undetermined amount of time. We stood in the background, watching like deer caught in headlights. The staff worked lovingly and patiently with him as he fought, screamed and cursed his way through the day. We followed him back to the apartment complex where the patients lived and we watched him fight every instruction he was given. In total exhaustion, we finally retreated to our hotel rooms. Everett and I said little before we went to sleep and watched some TV, trying to distract our minds from our reality. The pain was too deep for me to pray and I knew I was relying on the Holy Spirit, along with the prayers of my family, friends and church, to keep me on solid ground.

The next morning, we were to meet at the Centre and join Kevin and his counselor after they had spent an hour alone. Arriving at the Centre, we were informed they had been an hour late getting Kevin there as his aggression had continued throughout the night and morning and it had been difficult getting him there. What we saw when we finally walked into the counselor's office was not at all what we were expecting. Kevin was sitting calmly and quietly in his chair; it was the closest thing we had seen to the real Kevin in several months. The counselor was a no-holds-barred kind of guy and he told it like it was. What exactly transpired the hour before we came in we will never know, but I believe with all my heart it was a precious gift from God that we so desperately needed. From that moment on, there were no more physical or verbal assaults. This, however, did not mean that everything went smoothly from there on out.

Kevin lived more than seven months at the Centre and one, two, or more of us would travel to Bakersfield each weekend to spend time with him. Each month, as we met with his doctors, therapists and counselor, we learned more and more how damaged his brain really was and the limitations he would have for the rest of his life. The biggest problem was his eyesight. The trauma had all but destroyed the optic nerve. He was completely blind in his right eye, with only eight degrees of vision in his left—like looking through the end of a straw. His short-term memory was and is very poor and there were gaps in his long-term memory. He had vertigo and balance issues as well as some other minor cognitive disabilities. We were told it was quite likely he would never work again.

During the time Kevin was in a coma and throughout his time in acute rehabilitation, people were always telling me they just knew something wonderful was going to happen as a result of his accident. They felt Kevin was going to do wonderful things because God had said, "All things work together for good." One day a dear friend asked me if I had seen any good thing yet. I could only reply that I had not. Everyone's excitement about something wonderful yet to come only made me angry. I thought if one more person said that to me I was going to punch them and scream, "How could anything good possibly come of this?" I kept doubting my faith. Wasn't I strong enough to believe it? *"Why is everyone else so positive and I am not?"*

I was in so much emotional despair that I wasn't thinking clearly. Satan seized that opportunity to reinsert the lingering doubt in my mind once again as to whether or not I truly was God's child. This was a doubt I had kept buried deep inside, a niggling doubt I had about God, but thought I had settled once and for all in my heart and mind. I cannot tell you how many times through the years I had settled it "once and for all," but here it was again. Did I truly believe I belonged to Him? *"Oh, why do I continue to doubt?"* I was like the father in Mark's gospel who came to Jesus asking him to heal his son who was tormented by a demon and cried out to Jesus, "I believe, help my unbelief." Once again, I believe it goes back to the pain of my childhood. How do you trust a loving heavenly father when you have been so deeply emotionally wounded by an earthly father? Was I going to continue to let Satan feed me these lies and believe them?

When I would run into people who had or had not heard about Kevin's accident and they would ask me how he was doing, I would tell them and would try to be upbeat about it, but inside my heart was still breaking. Invariably they would smile and say, "Yes, but thank God he is alive and you still have your son." My gut reaction was to scream at them and say, "You don't know what you're talking about."

No one understood. My son had died that first day. No, not physically, but in a way I cannot justly describe. He was Kevin, but different. To me he didn't even look the same; there was an emptiness in his eyes that ripped at my heart. Maybe it was because of the blindness; I just don't know. He talked differently, moved differently. It was heartbreaking to ask him if he remembered an event from his past and he had no recollection of it. Skills he once had were forgotten or no longer allowed because they would be too dangerous for him.

Toward the end of January in 2008, we were told Kevin would be released soon and he would continue with some outpatient therapy. We were all ecstatic, but fearful of its implications. Would Kevin and Sarah be able to adjust to a new normal and keep their relationship good and strong? Could my husband and I get used to a new normal? I tried not to fear the worst, but there was a biting grief in my heart.

On January 25th, I had been working most of the day at our church, as I was the funeral coordinator and there was a memorial service that day for one of our dear ladies. I came home exhausted that evening and hit the couch. Maybe a half hour later the phone rang. I answered and a lady on the other end was telling me something absolutely impossible to believe. She and another friend of hers had just found my younger brother, Scott, dead in his apartment. He had committed suicide by using a shotgun to his head. Once again, my world disintegrated. After getting all the information I needed from her, I fell apart. My brother was dead and he was not with the Lord because he had openly refused to believe in God. In fact, he hated him.

How could this have happened? I had prayed for years that God would not let him die before he came to Christ. Why had God not honored those prayers? I knew why my brother didn't believe. It was for some of the same reasons I had struggled with. I know for him it had stemmed from an event in our lives that happened when he was only eight and I was nine. An event that happened at the hands of our father, an event that has haunted me all my life, an event my brother and I never spoke of, an event I believe traumatized him for the rest of his life, an event he alluded to in a suicide note.

My dad was pastoring a small country church in Illinois at that time. This particular day, the whole family was outside doing chores. At one point my dad realized Scott was nowhere around and a search began. My little brother was in the habit of escaping to a corner somewhere to read. Well, we found him down in the basement, cloistered in a corner, reading. My dad went ballistic. I don't remember the exact words but it went something like this, "What are you doing down here when everyone else is outside doing their chores? You're such a sissy little girl sitting in the corner reading a book. Well, if you want to act like a little girl you might as well look like one."

At that point he turned to me and yelled, "Tami, go upstairs and get your brother a dress to put on so he can be a little girl." You didn't argue with my dad so I ran upstairs to my room. I remember standing in front of my closet with tears streaming down my face wondering what I was going to pick out for my little brother to put on. I remember pulling out a little gray jumper and at that point the memory stops. I believe it was just too painful.

It was several days before I was allowed to enter my brother's apartment and pick up his personal effects from the coroner, as well as the notes he had left. As I read his short suicide notes—yes, notes—and his handwritten will, I couldn't help but notice God had spared me an even greater tragedy. His second suicide note stated he had attempted to take his life nine months earlier and had failed so he was taking more desperate means to complete the deed this time. His handwritten will and first note were dated May 6, 2007, one day before Kevin's accident. This explained why he hadn't answered the many calls and frantic messages I had left on his answering machine. I can only surmise he had tried to overdose on pills and lay in a deep sleep until he came to. I firmly believe God spared me his first attempt because He knew what was coming the next day and I couldn't have handled both things at once.

But here I was at the present. The family had been told Kevin would be released from the Centre in only a few weeks. After nearly ten months, Kevin was finally coming home. But I found myself mourning the death of my brother and angry, angry that I had to deal with my brother's suicide and the mess he had left behind. We had to get his filthy apartment cleared out and as we did, we discovered he had not opened mail in seven years. I later discovered he had not paid either his personal or business taxes in all those years as well. Kevin's homecoming was supposed to be a happy time, a time to celebrate, but instead, I was planning a memorial service for my brother and trying to figure out how I was going to take care of all his undone business.

I just wanted to run away and hide. My heart was breaking because of what my brother had done. I hadn't had time to really grieve what had happened to my son and now this was upon me. I cried out to God, "Just how strong do you think I am? I can't handle all this." Little did I know the trials weren't over. As funny as it sounds, I knew God was still trying to prove to me that He was there, I was His and that He was greater than all the difficulties in my life.

A short time later my husband and I began noticing odd things at church. Our new pastor was preaching things we didn't believe were quite biblical. He and the elder board were bringing things into the church we didn't believe belonged there. We were not alone in our concerns and after much prayer, many tears and months of trying to work things out, we felt God telling us it was time to leave.

This was unfathomable to me. My family had been there for twenty-six years. This was our home, our family whom we dearly loved. My husband and I had served in many different ministries there throughout all those years. We had weathered several difficult storms and had never felt quitting was an option. I had expected to be there the rest of my life. Sadly, the church split apart and most everyone left. This tore my broken heart even further apart. *"God, how can this be? What good can come of this?"* I cried for months. It felt like another death. My church family was spread throughout the surrounding communities to various churches and we were searching for a new church to call home.

This experience shook me to the very core of my being, but I also believe God used it to drive me out of my comfort zone. It tested my faith even more; it impacted my prayer life in a positive way. It drove me to pray more, to study His word more, to find more time alone with Jesus, to come closer to the God who loved me.

I needed to go deeper with God. I needed to diligently search the Scriptures. I needed to really pray. I couldn't go on living like this, with this silent fear I held onto so tightly, not allowing anyone to know. Everyone thought I had such a strong faith. I couldn't let anyone see I was a phony. No, I wasn't a phony, it was just that I couldn't let myself fully believe that God could love me, that He would want to grant His mercy to me, that He had washed me whiter than snow through His blood, granting me forgiveness and eternity with Him.

It was during the same time we were trying to work things out at our church that it became evident there was the great possibility my husband could lose his job. The company where he worked was being consolidated into one local plant, so there were many layoffs and it was rumored his department would be let go. Soon my husband was given notice that his department was indeed being closed and in thirty days he would be out of a job. At this same time, we received a doctor's diagnosis that he had prostate cancer. We scheduled his surgery to coincide with the end of his job. For some reason, I didn't seem to be worried or anxious about this and felt everything would be okay. Was I just numb or was God speaking peace to me? I chose to trust the later. All we could do was pray and ask God for his mercy and provision in all of this.

God had been working behind the scenes all along. We did not know that Everett's former supervisor, who had earlier left his department to take a better position at the new plant, had been tirelessly working to create a position for my husband in his department. Just a few days before Everett's scheduled surgery, we were informed this position had been approved and that it would be held open for him until he had recovered from his surgery, which would be about seven weeks.

God also abundantly provided for Everett's care. He had the top urologist at St. Jude Hospital performing his surgery. The hospital had a new robotic operating system and his doctor wanted him to be the first patient to have it. At first we were concerned that he was to be the guinea pig, but our fears were soon allayed when we found out the doctor and his surgery team had practiced hours upon hours making sure everything would go perfectly. Not until the day of the surgery did we learn representatives of the company who made the robot would also be in the operating room observing. So, we knew the surgeon would be super vigilant as he operated. Everett was the star patient and was treated like royalty. The doctor was able to remove all the cancer and Everett has remained cancer free.

Months after the breakup of our church, combined with everything else going on in my life, I found I was at a breaking point. I met with our new pastor and gave him the short version of my life and all the heartache going on inside of me. I was still reeling from the crisis of our church and I had never fully grieved my son's accident or the death of my brother. I had not had the time. But also, I would not allow myself to think about what had happened to our son and what implications it had on all our lives. I knew it would only reduce me to tears. For some unknown reason, I would not allow myself to go to that place. The pain of knowing my brother was not in heaven was too great. I couldn't understand why God had allowed it to happen. I felt as though I was coming apart at the seams.

At my new pastor's suggestion, I went off for a two-week period of time to spend alone with God without a television, radio, computer, or other distractions. I was both excited and pensive about two weeks of solitude. Though quite miserable with a case of bronchitis when the time came, my husband convinced me to go anyway. In a quiet cabin in the Big Bear Mountains, I not only tried to pour out my heart to God, but also tried to be still and listen for His voice.

I had never done anything like this before and it all felt quite awkward. I had brought with me several books written by A.W. Tozer and other great men of faith. As I read their incredible relationships with the Lord, it seemed to only make me feel more unworthy and that my faith was so very weak. I desperately wanted to sense God's presence the way they had. I would sit and read Scripture and tried to journal my thoughts and prayed to God. I was so overwhelmed with everything and I needed God's peace and joy so desperately. I prayed as best I could—trying to pour out all the pain and hurt and the many open wounds still fresh in my heart. "Oh God, you have lifted me out of the miry clay and set my feet on solid ground. How many times will you have to lift me out?" I cried. He would gently answer, "As many times as it takes."

I would sit for hours outside on the deck looking out at the clear blue sky, enjoying all the beauty of the pines, laughing at the antics of the squirrels and blue jays and praising God for the wonder of it all. As I enjoyed His creation, I would just sit and listen for His voice. Two weeks was not enough, but during those two weeks God began to finally break through the lies of Satan. God began to convince me that He loves me.

Once home, I continued to pursue God, or was He pursuing me? As I delved more into His word, the beauty of who I am in Christ came alive, fresh and new.

During the next two years, on several separate occasions, I was able to spend several weeks at my older brother and sister-in-law's house in the piñon pine forest outside Albuquerque, where I would sequester myself in a back room or in the forest and spend hours upon hours with God, letting my heart heal. The pain of losing my younger brother still haunted me.

Meditating upon Scripture one day, God led me to Romans 9:22-23 (ESV), which says, "What if God, desiring to show his wrath and make known his power, has endured with much patience vessels of wrath prepared for destruction, in order to make known the riches of his glory for vessels of mercy, which he has prepared beforehand for glory . . ." With tears streaming down my cheeks, I thanked God that He had made me a vessel of mercy. Still unable to understand the senselessness of my brother's death, I chose to trust God's wisdom, without knowing why. My brother had known the truth but had chosen not to accept it.

In 2008, my dad was living in Kentucky. Through a strange turn of events that would fill another chapter, he found himself divorced from his third wife. Because he was incapable of being completely on his own, he had to relocate to Albuquerque so my brother and sister-in-law could help take care of him.

My brother and I believe the events that led to Dad's divorce and move to Albuquerque were in answer to our prayers. We had been praying for years that God would use any means possible to bring Dad back to Jesus and we believe this was how He accomplished it. Dad's despair over the situation he had found himself in began his prodigal return to Jesus.

I would like to say that Dad had asked for forgiveness from his children. However, knowing that this was not in his character to do so, my brother and I had granted it to him anyway years earlier.

Sadly, Dad passed away quite unexpectedly and alone in his apartment February 2, 2011. Happily, I am now confident that Dad made his peace with God, that I will see him again in heaven and that all the brokenness of our lives will then be healed.

Kevin has come a long way since his accident and has amazed us all with his resilience. He has learned well to compensate for his disabilities and seems to have taken a lot of it in stride. However, it has not been easy for Kevin and Sarah, as many adjustments needed to be made and continue to be made. But they tackle each new obstacle, trusting God to see them through. Three years after Kevin's accident, Kevin and Sarah were blessed with a beautiful son, my first grandchild. To say he is the joy of my life is an understatement.

After four and a half years unable to work, God amazingly provided a job for Kevin that he has not only been able to do, but has excelled at. More and more responsibilities have been given to him. Sarah was able to leave her job and be the stay-at-home mom she has always wanted to be.

After a year into Kevin's new job, a car hit him as he was walking back to work after a lunch break. This time, however, my reaction was not panic. I felt a total calmness as Sarah called to tell me what had happened. A lady making a left-hand turn plowed into him in the crosswalk. He was tossed into her windshield, breaking it and then thrown some twenty feet down the road. With glass embedded in his face and skull and his head busted open, he was rushed to the hospital. After three days in the ICU he was able to return home with a stapled head, stitches in his face, a fractured knee and many bumps and bruises. By God's grace, there was no further damage to his brain. A month later, still not completely healed from the first accident, a man making a right-hand turn hit him once again in the crosswalk. He was knocked off his feet but got up and continued across the street to meet his ride to work. Once again, God was watching out for him. I can't honestly say these two incidents have not caused me any concern, but I can say I am trusting God and will keep trusting Him no matter what may lie ahead.

Did God cause all these bad things to happen? I don't believe that for a moment. Did He allow them? Yes. I now believe they were used for my own good, as only God can take the pain and junk of our lives and turn it into something beautiful; something useful for His glory. When these things stretched my faith almost to the breaking point and I finally yielded to God, I got a closer view of the Lord who promised to keep me securely in His hands and who loved me with an everlasting love. Romans 5:3-4 (ESV) says it best: ". . . we rejoice in our sufferings, knowing that suffering produces endurance and endurance produces character and character produces hope and hope does not put us to shame, because God's love has been poured into our hearts through the Holy Spirit who has been given to us."

Psalm 37:23-24 (ESV) says, "The steps of a man are established by the LORD, when he delights in his way; though he fall, he shall not be cast headlong, for the LORD upholds his hand." God, the author and finisher of my faith, has already written my story. My portion is to walk in the steps He has ordained for me, trusting Him through each difficult moment, knowing He will lead me and hold me up, giving me strength for each difficult step. I am assured He will keep me all the way to glory.

First Peter 1:6-9 (ESV) says, "In this you rejoice, though now for a little while, if necessary, you have been grieved by various trials, so that the tested genuineness of your faith—more precious than gold that perishes though it is tested by fire—may be found to result in praise and glory and honor at the revelation of Jesus Christ. Though you have not seen him, you love him. Though you do not now see him, you believe in him and rejoice with joy that is inexpressible and filled with glory obtaining the outcome of your faith, the salvation of your souls." This verse says, "if necessary you have been grieved by various trials." I do believe the trials of my life have been necessary— necessary to learn to know God, to trust God, to grow and strengthen my faith in Him and to convince me of His salvation.

I have discovered that joy for me is not a giggling, jumping up and down shouting "Hallelujah" sort of thing, but is instead a quiet gentle stream of assurance flowing in my heart and soul, keeping me in that perfect peace, because His hand is stayed on mine. Isaiah 26:3 (ESV) says, "You keep him in perfect peace whose mind is stayed on you, because he trusts in you." I like that word "stayed." Through all my trials and all my doubts and confusion, I am now confident that Christ's sure and loving hand was and is locked and stayed on mine. In spite of me, Jesus stayed.

Kathleen

"Have I not commanded you? Be strong and of good courage; do not be afraid, nor be dismayed, for the Lord your God is with you wherever you go." Joshua 1:9 (NKJV)

I can still clearly remember an event that changed the course of my life. At twenty years old, I was attending college, had a good job and was getting ready to move out with a friend. One fall morning, just before sunrise, my mother opened my bedroom door and in a frantic voice cried out, "Your father is having a heart attack!"

My dad rushed behind her and yelled, "Marie! Get in the car!" Amazingly, he drove himself to the emergency room. He was admitted and hospitalized for a month. During that time my mother slept in my room. She told me that they had not been apart since my dad was in the Navy during World War II.

The night before he came home, my mother, through her tears, told me she didn't want to live if he died. I was crushed. My mind reeled as I asked, "What about us?"

Through her sobs she explained, "You don't understand. I can't live without him!" Her words stunned me. Then, she lifted her shirt to show me her bloated stomach. In a solemn voice she stated, "I don't know what's wrong with me."

Flashes of childhood memories gripped me. My anxious thoughts crushed me, making it hard to breath. This was not the first time. Ten years before, Mom was diagnosed with breast cancer and underwent a mastectomy. My fear of losing her overwhelmed me, even after she came home from the hospital. At ten years old, in an attempt to calm my fear, I reasoned that if she died when I was an adult I would be okay. Those words came back and relentlessly played over and over in my head. I was not ready to let her go.

My mother was diagnosed with ovarian cancer that had metastasized. While she was in the hospital, as a family we began taking shifts visiting her. On my twenty-first birthday, my mom had an extra breakfast tray brought to her hospital room so we could eat together. We had a wonderful time just talking about our family and my plans for the day. Before I left, Mom pulled a card from her purse. Her eyes welled up as she put it in my hand. Her voice broke, "This is for you. I wanted to buy you something." My body stiffened as I fought back tears. She handed me some money, "Buy yourself something nice." We both wept.

That night she had a heart attack and a stroke. Out of the grace of God, her doctor was in the next room and able to treat her immediately, but it took him three hours to revive her.

When I arrived, Dad and my Aunt Doll, my mother's younger sister, were just coming out of ICU. With tears filling his eyes, Dad said, "She looks better." He made it to the men's room before completely falling apart; that was the first time I had seen my father cry.

My chest felt like it was in a vice; it was hard to breath. I asked if I could see her. Brushing away tears Aunt Doll replied, "Remember your mother the way she was." Then, she rushed in to the women's bathroom. My heart pounded. I found it hard to get enough air; I needed to see her. Dad finally agreed.

Seeing her in ICU with so many monitors and tubes was unsettling, but she was still my mother. Just seeing her somehow comforted me. Tears streamed down my face as I stood next to her bed. The strongest woman I knew looked so frail.

She recovered from the stroke, but her left side was partially paralyzed. Two months later the doctor's told us there was nothing more they could do.

Mom wanted to come home so my dad hired a nurse. It was comforting having her home again. We had many long talks. A couple weeks went by and we noticed she was getting weaker. Then she stopped eating.

Early one morning my dad got up and visited with Mom for a while. He pulled the nurse aside and asked her how Mom was doing.

The nurse said her breathing was less consistent than it had been but she could continue on for days or weeks. My dad went into the kitchen for a cup of coffee and when he returned, Mom was gone. It was a peaceful transition as she went to be with the Lord, another gift from God.

After hearing the news I sat next to her bed, tears streaming down my face. It felt surreal, numb. A sudden flood of panic rushed over me as I realized she was not in her body anymore. Then, I felt her presence in the room. It comforted and calmed me. In the next room there was a sense of urgency. My dad, brothers and sisters bustled in and out until the mortuary workers arrived. Another flood of panic rushed through me as they carried her body to a waiting car. It seemed so sterile, emotionless. I wanted the world to stop just for a day and mourn with me, but everything just kept going. How could God allow this? I felt God was unjust for taking my mother when I still needed her.

The day of her funeral, my boyfriend, who had been with me throughout her illness, broke up with me. My best friend stopped returning my calls and my grieving dad shut down emotionally. In my pain I felt lost, alone and abandoned by everyone, including God. I couldn't sleep. Grief flooded, like waves crashing relentlessly over my mind. Aching thoughts of loneliness choked me.

One day while driving, the pain was unbearable. I considered swerving into oncoming traffic, but the thought, "*I could hurt someone else too*" kept me from doing it. I sobbed in anguish, feeling hopeless. In desperation I reached out to my sister, Gloriann, who came home from work to be with me. "The angel of the Lord encamps all around those who fear Him and delivers them," (Psalm 34:7 NKJV). She was a gift from God that day.

Our family was close before my mother's death. There were nine of us and I was number eight. Mom had been the glue that had kept us together. After her death there were many years when our family felt broken. We were all grieving separately and in our own way. It took several years before we would figure out how to come back together as a family.

I started seeing a therapist. It was healing having someone listen to my story and validate my thoughts and feelings. During one session, the therapist cried with me as I talked about the many losses. I felt heard and understood. He helped me to see that my life experiences do not have to define me.

On my twenty-second birthday, my dad announced he was

143

getting married in a month. He and his new bride stayed in the house I grew up in, the house where our close family had celebrated holidays, birthdays and life accomplishments.

The next Christmas I realized how broken our family had become and again I felt alone. It was Christmas Eve, which we had always celebrated at my parents' house. I called the house and my stepmother answered. I asked what was happening for Christmas Eve. She told me she was having her family over and wasn't sure what I was going to do. I was stunned! I hung up the phone and sat dazed for a few minutes. For the first time, I was alone on Christmas Eve. I called my older sisters but they were busy with their families. I called my roommate at his mother's house. His brother answered the phone. He asked me what I was doing. I gasped and paused trying to fight back the flood of tears that was about to burst. I tried to remain composed but my tears came gushing out uncontrollably and I began to sob. His mother picked up the extension phone and the two consoled me. They invited me to spend Christmas Eve with their family. A memory I will never forget. They made me feel so welcome. "For you will light my lamp; the Lord my God will enlighten my darkness," (Psalm 18:28 NKJV) I would realize later this was another gift from God.

As I left that night, I looked across the street at the house I grew up in. There were lights on and unfamiliar cars in the driveway. My dad had moved on and had a new family that I needed to adjust to. Now I had a stepmother and six stepsiblings. Her thirty-year-old son lived with them. He made my old room into a Black Sabbath shrine, complete with posters and black lights. Her daughters lounged by our family pool and I was not invited over. I couldn't go back. It was no longer my house.

A few months later I met evil. I decided to have a party at my apartment but many of my friends couldn't make it. While sitting at work contemplating whether to postpone the party, a coworker walked in. He began making his case about why I should have the party anyway, stating he would bring the refreshments. All I had to do was provide the place. Then he looked at me and asked, "Don't you trust me, Kathy?"

Every bone in my body screamed, "NO!" Not listening to my gut feeling, I decided to have it. The night of the party the coworker brought a friend and some wine. My best friend was there. The last thing I remember before blacking out was having a glass of wine and feeling like something wasn't right. I glanced at the clock and saw

9:00 p.m.

Thinking I was dreaming, I heard someone talking but the voice echoed and I was having trouble understanding his words. Quickly the dream turned to a nightmare, my worst nightmare! It took me a few minutes to realize what was happening. I was being raped! It's hard to describe my feelings, violation, helplessness, vulnerability and fear for my life. I knew of this man's anger, having seen him go off on a co-worker, so I knew better than to upset him. I looked at the clock: 2:00 a.m. Disgusted by the situation, I started vomiting on him. He got up and washed in my bathroom. I felt relief for a moment but then he came back in and lay next to me. I wanted to scream, but fear took my voice captive. I lay compliantly still next to him, my heart violently pounding in my chest. He left before sunrise. I continued to lay still, feeling numb, dazed.

The next morning my sister Dori called. Feeling surreal, with no emotion, I told her what happened. She yelled, "You were raped!"

I remember saying, "I just want it to go away." I lay curled up in a ball, wrapped in a blanket on my bed until the following day, just hoping to wake up from this horrible nightmare. I called a rape hotline. The kind woman on the other end tried to convince me it wasn't my fault but I couldn't shake off the condemning thoughts swirling around in my head. I had invited him over. I had let him into my house. Somehow I deserved it. God couldn't love me.

The following Monday at work the man asked me not to tell anyone what had happened. A mixture of fear and anger overwhelmed me. He had attacked me! Would he try again? Words stuck in my throat as I tried to speak. Unable to look at him I stared at the floor. Feeling embarrassed and defeated, I turned and walked away. I became acutely aware when he was around and tried to avoid him whenever possible, giving him no eye contact. Several times he waited for me in the parking lot after work but I avoided him. It was exhausting, planning ways to evade him, waiting for him to give up, walking out with others so he would leave me alone. My thoughts of that horrific night haunted me, making it hard to focus at work, at home, anywhere. His actions changed my life forever. Why did he attack me? I needed to know.

One day after work as he approached me in the parking lot, I decided to confront him. He wanted to talk to me. We agreed to meet at a local restaurant, driving separately there. When I arrived he was sitting at a table, one glass and a pitcher of beer in front of him. I confronted him, "Why me?"

"I wanted you to know what it was like to be with a real man," he replied.

"I wasn't there," I retorted. "Didn't you notice? I was passed out."

Growing angry he threatened, "Next time, you'll be awake."

Trying to stay strong, I announced, "You'll never get me again." My skin crawled and my body felt paralyzed with fright as I stared at his cold dark eyes. Thoughts of evil clouded my mind.

In the middle of my thoughts he announced, "I have a gun in my car. If you cross me, if you tell anyone, I will go to the ends of the earth to find you; and I will kill you. I am the devil," he added. "You mean nothing to me."

I sat motionless in my fear. He finished his beer and left. Still trembling from the conversation, I left.

I tried hard to go on with my life, to avoid the disturbing thoughts by keeping busy. Then, three months later, in my office desk drawer, I found pictures of his body and a note that stated what he intended to do to me next time. I could not contain my emotions. I burst into tears and ran straight to security. Trembling I handed the note and pictures to two security guards. I told them the story. Defensively, they stated, "We can't be sure it was him."

Shocked, I went home sobbing. Again I lay on my bed wrapped in a blanket. It was happening all over again! This time others knew and they didn't care.

No longer feeling safe anywhere, having nightmares and afraid to be alone, I couldn't sleep. Fear consumed me, making simple daily tasks difficult. Seeing a therapist helped, but the assailant's haunting threats viciously repeated in my head. It wasn't over. He knew where I lived. It could happen again! Still feeling victimized and wanting to gain control back in my life, I decided to speak up. I met with the assailant's boss, who happened to be a Christian. After telling my story his boss fired him and had him escorted off the premises. He demonstrated God's love and care for me. Looking back, there was God again intervening. I know God protected me from a situation that could have been so much worse and ongoing.

Having him fired gave me some sense of power but I also feared he would retaliate. That fear kept me always looking over my shoulder. Unable to live by myself, I moved in with my boyfriend, whom I thought would protect me if the assailant ever came after me again.

That fear kept me imprisoned and my world grew smaller. Then one day a friend invited me to a Bible study and to church. I remember feeling comfort and security there and really wanting to know more about God, but still being a little cautious, thinking God was judging me and I was not good enough for His love. After all, I was living with my boyfriend, something I knew was wrong.

The Bible study gave me a glimpse of God's love for me. My thoughts of God were conflicted though. I was thankful to God that the rapist did not kill me, but I also felt God was punishing me, that somehow it was my fault.

I went to see my therapist again and over time, I was able to talk about the trauma I had endured. He taught me healthy ways to handle my anxiety. He also helped me build my self-confidence and to learn to listen to my gut. Eventually I was able to live on my own.

Therapy was helpful but I still struggled with trust and fear.

At twenty-five, I met my first husband. We hit it off from our first date, having many interests in common. He had recently found the Lord and had joined a Christian church. We began attending together. I felt this was where I needed to be. I wanted to learn all about God. Our relationship developed rapidly and he proposed to me about a year after we met. His family was close, like mine used to be and it was comforting to be part of a family again. It felt good. We had a big beautiful wedding with all our family and friends present.

While on our honeymoon I began having abdominal pain. The doctor ordered an ultrasound that showed a mass sitting in my lower abdomen. He put me on antibiotics, hoping it was an infection. But after five days there was no change. The doctor explained that he would need to surgically remove the tumor. The possibility of me having cancer like my mother scared me.

After surgery, I was told he had to remove two tumors. One was attached to my left ovary and the other was in my uterus, but the doctor quickly reassured me that neither was cancerous. He stated the right ovary looked good so I should be able to have kids. I thanked God for His blessings that day.

Six months later a cyst appeared on my right ovary. The first doctor wanted to remove it. I prayed and pleaded with God. Having children was one of my dreams. By His grace we found another doctor for a second opinion. He diagnosed me with a thyroid problem and I began taking medication. In a couple of weeks the cyst disappeared. I was able to conceive and my son CJ was born a year later. I thank God for answering my prayers and for His gift, a precious son!

When CJ was a month old, he was hospitalized for an infection.

My heart pounded so hard from the news, it made it difficult for me to think straight, but I had to stay focused to help my son. He was given antibiotics through an IV. I prayed for the Lord not to take him so soon, hoping God was listening. My relationship with God was better, but we were not close and I lacked faith and trust in Him.

The hospital brought in a cot and I slept next to his crib. On the second day I noticed his arm swelling under the big bandage that was securing the IV. The vein had collapsed and they had to change the IV to the other arm. Two days later the same thing happened with his other arm. He only had one day left for the antibiotics. A neonatal nurse was brought in to put the IV into his head. They made us leave the room but we could hear CJ crying. My heart broke. I felt helpless. CJ's aunt, grandmother, father and I knelt in a circle and began to pray until the nurse came out. She saw us praying and told us she was a Christian. Then she explained how she had assessed him and could not find a vein to use, so she called his doctor and recommended giving the last two doses by a shot. At the end of the week the infection was gone! The Lord answered our prayers. Once again God was there, working behind the scenes.

My brother Mike was diagnosed the following year with a malignant brain tumor. I felt numb. Mike, who was two years older than I, was my protector and my hero. Since he was young and in good shape, I reasoned, he was going to beat it. Besides, he had two beautiful children and his wife, whom he loved, was pregnant, so God would not take him away now!

A year later my precious daughter Chelsea was born. She was another gift from God! Shortly after her birth, I gave my life to the Lord. For the first time I felt safe and truly loved. My husband and I were baptized together in a lake by our home with our friends and two children present. We were happy! My life was complete! Now that I was saved, everything would be okay. God was on our side and nothing bad would happen from now on; or so I thought.

I was blessed again when God used me to lead Mike to the Lord before he died. The last conversation we had is still fresh in my mind. All morning he spoke clearly about God and how everything was going to be okay. His words were comforting. He sounded so sure of God and the future. A few weeks later, at the age of thirty-four, Mike went to be with the Lord.

After his death my faith faltered. I thought he was going to be okay. Why did God take Mike? His family needed him! He was too young to die! I joined a hospice support group and met some wonderful people who had also lost loved ones.

Within months after Mike's death, my marriage began to crumble and two of my brother-in-laws passed away. Overwhelmed with grief, I felt distraught and confused. How could God turn His back on our family? I was saved! Things were supposed to turn out okay. Feeling desperate, I took my eyes off the Lord and filed for divorce, hoping my husband would miss me enough to work things out, but that didn't happen. I realized the flaws in my logic years later.

After our divorce was final, I felt hurt and angry with God. Why did He allow this? Starting over and learning to do everything on my own was hard. My son was seven and my daughter was five when we moved into a two-bedroom apartment while my ex-husband kept the house. I had to buy a small used car because I couldn't afford the payments on the SUV I had been driving. Working and taking care of my kids left me feeling tired most of the time. I had been a stay at home mom and loved it. That was gone. Going to events alone and celebrating holidays without my children every other year was difficult.

Through that pain I felt God's presence. The Lord whispered comforting things to me, but I let my old fears get the best of me after my ex-husband told me he realized we were never meant to be and that he had found someone else. The old negative thoughts about myself were back. It was over. I was replaceable; I was unlovable. I lacked trust and faith in God and His plans for my life. God whispered, *"Just hold on,"* but I panicked. Negative thoughts flooded my mind. *"How am I going to raise two children on my own? I'm a mess!"*

Fear got the best of me again and I married a man I did not love. He seemed to treat my children well at first. The day of our wedding I knew this wasn't God's plan for my life, but I was afraid to be alone. He was not a Christian and after we were married he stopped going to church with us. The Scripture, 2 Corinthians 6:14, which warns against being unequally yoked with an unbeliever, had new meaning.

A few months later I walked in on my husband yelling at my son. His verbal abuse towards us became more frequent. We decided to separate. One day before we moved out, I happened to come home early. He was on the phone with another woman making a date. He told me he was moving on with his life. After we moved out he cancelled my insurance but the Lord was with me. I remember going to the same doctor who had diagnosed my thyroid problem, for a checkup. After hearing I was a single mom again he gave me a year's supply of my medication from samples. Another blessing from God!

My second marriage ended after only two years. Now I had two failed marriages behind me and I was the common denominator. That was when I realized my brokenness and need for my Savior. I started attending church again and rededicated my life to the Lord. I had blamed God for my first marriage ending and all the problems that followed, but now I knew God doesn't promise us an easy life just because we are saved. Joining a divorce support group helped me process both marriages. God became my protector, close friend and heavenly Father. "And those who know your name will put their trust in you; For you, Lord have not forsaken those who seek you," (Psalm 9:10 NKJV).

At age thirty-nine, I was a single mom again. There were many hard times, like being at church and seeing my children with their dad and his wife. They were this happy little family, another reminder that I was replaced. But as I studied the Bible and fellowshipped with other believers, I realized that I am loved just the way I am, with all my good and bad parts. That, in God's eyes, I am irreplaceable. God says in Psalm 139:14 that, "I am fearfully and wonderfully made."

My job as a graphic artist worked well with my children's school and activities until the company began to grow. When they asked me to work longer hours, I decided to quit. Before the divorce I was a stay at home mom and loved it, so not seeing my children everyday was difficult for me. I remember praying to God for direction for a new job. Then I opened the classified ads and came across an interesting job as a reading teacher. To my surprise it was at my children's school. The principal offered me the job over the phone and I started the next day. It was only a part time job and low paying but the Lord provided for us and it gave me a chance to see my children more often. "And my God shall supply all your need according to his riches in glory by Christ Jesus," (Philippians 4:19 NKJV). Another blessing from God!

With God's help and guidance, I went back to school and received my bachelor's degree. This allowed me to teach full time and to earn a decent salary. Isaiah 58:11 says, "The Lord will guide you always; he will satisfy your needs in a sun-scorched land and will strengthen your frame." He was with me, taking care of our needs. I have told others I got through school, paid the bills and took care of my children by the grace of God.

As a single mom, money was tight. There were times when I was barely able to pay the bills, so extra things like vacations were not in my budget. There was one time when I was able to save enough money for us to spend one night at the Disneyland Hotel. My sister Gloriann and her son Robert also spent the night with us. It was the day before the grand opening of California Adventure Park, so they gave us free passes for the new park. We had such a wonderful time, all smashed into a hotel room with two beds and a cot. Those memories are so special to me. My children have reminded me of that trip many times over the years. One more time when the Lord provided for us!

Two years later on a Friday night, I was sitting at home correcting papers when the phone rang. My children were with their father so I was alone. A woman from a dating service asked me if I would like to come in and talk to her about joining. I told her I would never do that. She said, "Well you're sitting home on a Friday night."

"She's right," I thought. So I went in the next day and after three hours and much prayer, I signed up.

Three months after joining I was already tired of it. I decided there was only one guy I would go out with if he called. I had picked Larry and was waiting for his response. He accepted my offer, but the office had messed up and put down that he had declined my invitation. Larry happened to go in to watch my video before he called me, when he noticed the mistake. Looking back, I'm convinced that was another divine intervention. I remember answering the phone when Larry called and thinking sarcastically, "Oh, great; another one." I was cold as I asked his name, then I went flipping through the bios I had. When I came across his, I was pleasantly surprised!

We hit it off right away. Larry was not saved when we met so I was skeptical about getting too involved. I did not want to be unequally yoked again. Larry attended church with us on Sundays. Then I invited him to Greg Laurie's Harvest Crusade at Anaheim Stadium. To my surprise, when Greg Laurie gave his altar call Larry went down on the field. I just kept praying and thanking God. We became engaged shortly after that.

We were married a year later and have been married for over ten years. I believe the Lord picked Larry for me. God has shown me how to love again and has given me a loving partner. Larry is funny, patient and kind. We love spending time together, watching movies, going to church, golfing, taking long walks, or just sitting and talking. Larry has been wonderful with CJ and Chelsea and they have both grown to love him very much, as Larry does each of them. Two years after we were married, CJ said that Larry was a great guy and that he loves him. Chelsea told me Larry remembers so many things about her that make her feel special.

God filled in the gaps caused by my sins and helped me to forget the past. He says in Isaiah 43:18-19, "Forget the former things; do not dwell on the past. See, I am doing a new thing! ...I am making a way in the wilderness and streams in the wasteland."

Like in Jeremiah 29:11, one of my favorite passages in the Bible, God's plans for my life are much better than any of mine. This revelation came to me just after I started graduate school to become a marriage and family therapist at age forty-nine. I was working part time and we were feeling stretched financially. Then I was laid off, but the Lord still provided for us. During my time in school, I was humbled as I learned about more of my shortcomings. In this season of my life I have learned a lot about grace, forgiveness and letting go of the past. His plans are better than any I could imagine.

Shortly after starting grad school, I remember getting news about my friend and sister, Nancy. It came as a shock since the last I had heard was that she was in the hospital for a hysterectomy and doing fine. I had turned off my phone while in a doctor's appointment. On my way home I turned my phone on and found I had several messages. I remember hearing Nancy's voice. She sounded good but there was something in her tone that caught my attention. At the end of her message she told me to call her. There was a pang in my stomach as I called her back. Her voice was calm as she explained that she was feeling okay but that they found a small spot on one of the ovaries they had removed that was cancer. My mind raced as thoughts of my mother's illness rushed into my mind and swirled around relentlessly. Tears streamed down my face as I tried to stay focused on the road.

I remember going with her to the doctor. We sat in the doctor's office together and I had told myself I was going to be strong for her. This was so hard for me because we are so close. The doctor began telling us about the chemo treatment and then about the side effects. As he got to the part about her losing her hair my eyes began to well up. The thought of all the side effects she was going to have to endure was painful to hear. She looked at me and we both started to cry. The doctor was wonderful, very kind and caring. I remember taking her to one of her treatments. She was so gracious. Nancy talked to the patients around her and made them feel special.

Then, just before mid-terms, my brother, Frank, called and asked if I could come help him and his girlfriend. Frankie had diabetes and problems with his heart. I was overwhelmed with school and all my responsibilities at the time and was scheduled to give a presentation at school on a volunteer client who kept canceling on me. When I asked the teacher for more time she said no. So when Frankie called, I told him I could not come over that weekend but I could help the following weekend. I struggled with that decision. Sunday night Frankie called and said he just wanted to talk and that he didn't expect me to fix things. Then he proceeded to tell me that lately he had not been feeling well and that tomorrow he would go to dialysis and be weak that night and then by Tuesday he would have a heart attack. Frankie explained that he had already lived his "heyday" and now had those memories to think about. He also talked about our family stories and how much we meant to him. When I hung up the phone I turned to my husband and said, "I think Frankie just told me he was going to die soon."

Tuesday morning I called Frankie and told him I could come over to see him the next day. Frankie told me not to come. He said everything was going to be fine and that he had been up all morning telling our family stories to his girlfriend. I went to school and during our break, Larry came walking into my classroom. I remember thinking, *No, that's not my husband, because if it is then something really bad has happened.* I felt numb as he told me the news; Frankie had died from a heart attack.

The next day my sisters, Nancy and Dori, my niece, Kim and I all drove to my dad's house to tell him about Frankie in person. God was with us that day as Nancy told him the news in such a gracious way. Then, we all wept together. Before we left, my dad thanked us and said that it was the best way for him to get the news.

Shortly after starting my last year of grad school my father became very ill and we, as a family began taking shifts to take care of him. There were so many things that had to be done, like finding a nursing home for him and then taking shifts at the nursing home to make sure he was getting proper care. The dean of my graduate program, Geri, was so helpful. She listened and prayed with me and allowed me grace in my last few classes.

I wouldn't have done anything differently. The time I spent with my father was precious and healing. I was able to see my father's strengths and how God was working in all our lives. He went to be with the Lord during my last semester. The night he died, we, his family, were all gathered around the bed. Dori, the youngest in the family, stood holding his hand. As Dad took his last breath, he lifted his arm and squeezed Dori's hand as if to say, "I love you and I will see you again." He continued squeezing her hand until his arm dropped and he was gone. We were all amazed and felt so blessed to have had such a wonderful father and to have been able to experience his peaceful transition to be with the Lord.

My teachers were very gracious and once again the Lord carried me through my classes and I was able to graduate. As with all God's plans, I earned my master's degree through His grace and strength. Now, I am a marriage and family therapist intern at SPARE Counseling in Anaheim, California. My life experiences have given me compassion, empathy and a heart for families, single parents, blended families and individuals struggling with anxiety, depression and the loss of a loved one.

Sometimes God closes doors even when we are not ready for the change. He uses hard times to make us stronger in faith and character. Life with the Lord is a journey that is filled with blessings, trials and sorrows.

The biggest lesson I've learned is that I can't do anything worthwhile without His power and His blessing on it. I have also learned that when something is in God's will it doesn't happen in my time frame, but it happens when He decides and without much effort on my part.

Out of the grace of God both my children know the Lord and are finding their personal journey with Him. I have an amazing son, CJ, who graduated from U.C.I. and works as a liaison to America for a game company in Tokyo, Japan. My beautiful daughter, Chelsea, also graduated from U.C.I. She is a wonderfully talented seamstress, costume designer, make-up artist and hair stylist. I am so proud of both my children. Can you tell?

The trials in my life have brought me spiritual growth, which I am grateful for, but I would never want to go through those trials again. That being said, I know there will be more trials for me to endure, but I also know that God will be with me. I focus on Philippians 4:8, which says "Finally, brothers, whatever is true, whatever is noble, whatever is right, whatever is pure, whatever is lovely, whatever is admirable—if anything is excellent or praiseworthy—think about such things." I try to be content in every situation. Someday I will be in Heaven with God and all my loved ones that have gone before me,.

Gloriann

*There I will give her back her vineyards and will make the
Valley of Achor a door of hope. There she will sing as in the days
of her youth, as in the day she came up out of Egypt.*

Hosea 2:15

Alone but Not Alone

It was January 1997 and it had been a very long day of waiting
rooms and medical tests. I brought my husband, Phil, home and he
laid down to rest. Quietly, I slipped away to the den of our beautiful
home and closed the door. I called my friend, Suzie, and she prayed
with me for a while. I threw myself on the floor, arms outstretched
and cried out to God, "I can't do this!"

In my life there were only two times before that I heard the voice
of God in silence. It was not the audible voice that can be a sign of
mental illness but the still, quiet stirring in my spirit. He said, *"This is
going to be hard. It will be the hardest thing you ever had to do. But I will be with
you and you will be okay."*

Within minutes, another friend knocked at my front door. It was
a young woman I worked with at the Gas Company. A few years
before, her husband had suffered a brain tumor. Disabled since his
surgery, he had become suicidal. The Lord used me to introduce
Himself to her and her husband and they accepted Him. And now
here she was, on my front porch. She said, "I was driving by and the
Lord said you needed me. It was the strangest thing. Are you all

155

right?" This was an amazing confirmation that, indeed, I was not alone.

ಬುಗ

On our seventeenth wedding anniversary (May 10, 1997), our last together, we sat in Mimi's restaurant. Phil was a few weeks shy from his forty-sixth birthday. Neither of us realized that he had less than two and half months to live. He asked me if I would care for him.

"Of course," I responded without hesitation.

He said, "But last week you said that for a nickel you would leave."

"Well," I told him, "I can't guarantee that I won't have any more tantrums, but I will take care of you." He looked relieved.

In the weeks to come we were closer than ever before. He bravely tried to show us everything he could about the yard and the house. I prayed with him when he was in pain. I prayed for him when he slept. I cared for him with all my strength. All was forgiven and only the love remained.

I could not have taken care of him by myself. Phil's mother, siblings and his doctor (a close friend of the Connor family) all were wonderful. My sister-in-law, Vivian, called and offered a lot of support with resources and advice about options for nursing care. I had so many friends who really helped, not only by helping and visiting, but also by taking our kids and helping them. My sister, Joanie, and my niece, Jennifer, really took over during the last week, making meals, giving shots and taking phone calls.

Joanie had just lost her husband a month before, but she had always been the Florence Nightingale on my side of the family. I remember when Phil was still mobile and I came back from an errand. I saw Phil jumping up and down and motioning at someone in the front yard as I drove in the back gate. He had Joanie on a ladder washing the outside of the house in his work boots. I took one look at her and started yelling at him, "She just lost her husband and you are making her wash our windows?!" I was so angry and he had the guiltiest look. Then he went outside alone. Joanie leaped off the ladder and told me to go outside and apologize to him that minute. We still laugh about that today.

It was only a few days later that I took Phil to the doctor and the doctor told me to take him home. He asked me what I had been told about Phil's condition at his last treatment before he transitioned to

156

hospice. I told him that I was told he had about six months to live. The doctor told me that he had only a week to ten days.

The next day Phil asked the children what he could do for them while he still could. Our son, Robert, said that he did not know how to grow things and he wanted to learn. Phil had me take them all to the nursery. They picked out some plants and Phil took them to the back yard and began digging. Before long, eleven-year-old Robert left and went to a friend's house. Phil came in and said, "I don't understand. You know, I can't do this anymore." By that time he was leaning over the sink. I helped him to the bed and told him not to worry, that he had done enough. He never really got up after that except to go for short walks.

The night before he went into a coma he danced with me. The next morning his last words to me were, "You did a really good job and I really love you, but I got to go now." His last gesture was a smile for me, but in his last moments I was struck with how precious and beautiful he was. My sister, Joanie, and my best friend, Beverly, were at my side when Phil slipped away. I know how lucky I am to have these memories to keep.

ಬಂಗ

Blessed in Sorrow

> *"This is what the LORD says, he who made the earth, the LORD who formed it and established it—the LORD is his name: 'Call to me and I will answer you and tell you great and unsearchable things you do not know.'"*
>
> Jeremiah 33:2-3

Unsearchable: hidden things unknown to me. Would the Lord really restore me in ways that are nothing short of incredible, as He did for Israel in the thirty-third chapter of Jeremiah? My husband struggled in life, as we all do, but he died with great courage and dignity. Sixteen days after his death I wrote, "My whole being aches. I know God is here somewhere, but I feel disconnected and alone" (*A Widow's Prayers*). After all was said and done, I loved Phil with all my heart. I was devastated; seventeen years of marriage was not enough. Trying to figure it out was useless. I was a forty-two year old widow. This was never the plan I envisioned.

So I began to write a journal that was later published by my church in a pamphlet. I am glad that I have those writings as they help me to recall how far I've come. "I can't believe he's gone. I miss his smile, our talks on the front porch at night and making love to him. I am so proud that I could take care of him and that is my greatest comfort. I am still so very sad that I will never see him again.

For years I took for granted that he would always be there. I see a picture or a rose on the bush that he planted on our anniversary and I want to cry. I want to tell him a joke and then I remember that he won't be home tonight. There will be no more family meals with the four of us, no more shared holiday gatherings, no more kisses and hugs. The great dark hole of sadness in my being says I will never pass this way again. A part of me has died and the rest of the world goes on. Nobody gets it. Time goes by and the telephone calls from friends decrease. Visitors are few and far between. Sooner or later it is God and I. Patiently He has waited to hold me. He has already forgiven my anger with Him for letting my husband die. He seeks an invitation, a call to Him. The only truth that cannot be lost is Him. I collapse into His love like a baby tired of fighting the sleep." (*A Widow's Prayers*)

I continued to write, finding it a useful outlet to express my feelings. This was the poem I wrote for Phil in 1998:

It has been more than six months
It has been only moments. It has been eternity.
Your scent lingers in your clothes, still in your closet.
Your heart lingers in your son's courage.
Your love lingers in the beauty of your daughter.
You have danced with me in moonlit dreams.
You have kissed me in twilight sleep.
Every parting word and deed have been shared,
Time after Time with tears of anguish.
Bravely you faced leaving the life you loved.
Bravely I must face the life you left behind.
Somewhere inside my spirit you know
A place we will always share.
We were lovers, we were sinners, we were friends.
We were married till death did us part.
I knew you in every sense of the word.
I loved you in every way one loves.
I know you forgave all my faults and wrongs.
Today I accept that forgiveness as truth.

You know all was forgiven as I laid you to rest.
I thank you for all that you were and all you gave.
You did a good job, I really love you,
But I need to go on now until we meet again,
Let the time and space between be filled up
With love and God...Goodbye, Phil.

Struggling with my feelings has been a big part of my widowhood. Jealousy and bitterness are two of the biggest adversaries I have faced since the death of my husband. I think that for me, recognizing them as the enemy was (and still is) one of my greatest challenges. It takes all my concentration to stay this course. It takes all my faith not to give up.

Once, on a bad day, I wrote this:

I remember July 4, 1997, eating watermelon with Phil and my friend, Karen, and her husband. I was 42 years old, he was 46. He would be gone by July 25. This year on July 4, 2013, it has been sixteen years. I did not realize I could still have a very bad grief day. Today I don't know how to get better, so I don't think I have anything really important to share or tell you. I am very tired and I know my kids are doing fine and they have been able to move on in their lives. But I think I am slowly giving up. Everything seems too hard and it's an effort just to get out of bed. I can muster the energy to go to work and be there for my clients, but I am feeling so broken. I try not to let Robert know, he has a whole life to live and the best is all in front of him, Katy and Erik too. But I am just spent. This is when I pray and I do things I don't feel like doing such as taking a shower, calling a friend, writing in my journal and not giving in to the pain one more time."

A few days later I wrote:

"I am sitting here with my cup of coffee and writing. The sky is blue with fluffy white clouds. I can see it from my desk. It reminds me of the day we got married. The weather was perfect. There was just the slightest breeze. Everyone looked amazing and everyone seemed happy: My mom, my dad, my brothers, Mike and Frank, my sister-in-law, Vivian, my brother-in-law, Jim. Those people are all gone now, but it was a blessed moment when they were all there with me and I was the star of the show. This is sweet grief: a treasure that I keep. It is no wonder that I would never want to completely "move on with my life". Yes it is sixteen years later. It is morning and I am doing OK. I slept well last night; my dog, Phoebe, is lying on the floor looking at me. I can hear my son talking on the phone outside on the porch. This is a good day. Honestly, most of my days are somewhere in between.

Grief and Guilt

Another emotion that has been part of widowhood is guilt; not about my care for Phil, but about many other things.

In the early days of my widowhood, I became aware that I secretly felt I was being punished for the terrible sins of my youth. It had been a long time since I thought about the abortions.

On January 22nd, 1973, the United States changed forever. I was still in high school. There was a Supreme Court Case (Roe v Wade) that affirmed a woman's "right to abortion," later to be called "a choice." I bought into the full-blown agenda of the "Women's Rights Movement." As I entered my college years, I was known as a "woman's libber" and took pride in it. Most of us young baby boomer college students did the same thing. Today, I am not a political person. I am very moderate in most of my views and I do avoid the political debates I used to thrive on. But having an abortion put me right in the middle of the most polarizing issue of the last hundred years. So much more than that, it made me face the differences between my own core values, my political attitudes, my expressed philosophical ideologies and my often irresponsible behaviors. It cut to the core of me and never really healed until I faced it.

The first abortion was the result of a date rape in May 1975. Some would say that rape is the exception. I never really even considered having that child. One of my sisters took me to a clinic. It was a cold white room. I remember a big black and white clock on the wall. So this was "Planned Parenthood." I don't remember where it was, but I know it was in Los Angeles somewhere. I had filled out some forms and given them a urine sample. I wasn't sure what to think, but I was scared.

160

A woman came out and said something like, "So how do you feel about being pregnant?"

There was no discussion of options; she was ready to "take care of this" the same day. I wasn't. But I made an appointment and found myself at a clinic in Inglewood about a week later. I only remember a few things clearly. One was being led to a room and examined by a doctor who pronounced me "seven weeks." Another thing was how cold everyone was. I think it was all so new that many of the providers were as uncomfortable with the procedures as the patients. I was wheeled out to the hallway on a gurney and lined up behind several other patients waiting their turn. At some point I was given an IV, but when I was taken into the room I was still very awake. I saw a glass container that seemed to have blood and tissue. They started the procedure and I screamed and the doctor yelled at the nurse, "She is awake?!"

The nurse looked at my swollen arm and saw that the solution had not gone into the vein and was infusing into my arm instead. They fixed it and I don't remember anything after that except waking up in the recovery room and my arm aching terribly. I did not talk about it again to anyone for some time. I did not want to date for several months, but then I went the other way and became very promiscuous.

But I came to believe that she was, in fact, a child; an innocent soul, now in the presence of the Lord. I named her Deborah Christine.

Deborah was my judge in a sense. She made me look at myself and was part of the road that led me to a relationship with Jesus Christ. I knew of Him, but did not know Him until about a year after the first abortion.

It was the fall of 1975 when I met a young man in geography class. I thought he was planning to ask me for a date, but instead he took me outside to tell me his story. When he did this it was like he was touching me in ways only God could have known and I was open as only the Holy Spirit could accomplish. I gave my heart to Jesus that day. The first few months God sent several people to minister to me. As the "pink cloud" of a new Christian faded, I began to backslide in a big way. I was in a sorority and partying often.

Not long after that I began dating a boy from a fraternity at school. By March, 1977, I was having sex with him and became pregnant again. This was different. I thought I loved him. I wanted to make the first abortion right by doing the right thing. I was in a tug-of-war with myself and my close friends and family. My boyfriend told me he did not want to be a father and that if I had the baby he would have nothing to do with me or it. He took me to have the abortion in May, 1977. My little sister told me that I looked very different when I came back. I was shut down and pretending that nothing happened. I occasionally spoke to a priest about it, but I really believed that I had committed the unforgivable sin and most of the time I lived in denial.

I was married in 1980 and the feelings of being pregnant brought back some of the pain of the past. Bringing a child into the world made it more real and I did many things to try to shut off the pain. Mostly, I ran away for many years. I had a very difficult time with my attachments to my two living children.

When Phil died in 1997, the pain of losing my husband seemed to open an old wound of grief. I participated in many ministries for post abortion women to heal. I had to understand that these two abortions were children, not just fetuses. And, they were not just any children; they were my children. Finally, I was responsible for ending their lives. I had to break the denial, I had to embrace the pain, I had to grieve to say goodbye and to let go. This was accomplished with prayer, writing letters to them and sharing the support of others. I named my children and memorialized them. My sister drew a picture of them as babies. I claimed them and released them to God. It brought me to a deeper understanding of how merciful God is and how terrible my sin was. I better understand why the price Jesus paid for me was so high.

I stood in the gap between the pro-choice and pro-life politics and reached out to the women (1 in 3) who were wounded on the front lines. I called that ministry "Wisdom's Children."

My second child's name was Matthew David. Matthew means a gift. Claiming him allowed me to fully receive the gift of unconditional love from the Lord. I gave him the middle name of David because David was a "man after God's own heart."

Who knows what my life would have been like if those two lives were not lost. Today (in 2014), Deborah would be 39 and Matthew would be 37.

I always believed that I was meant to be a single parent for at least part of my life. When Phil died so young, that calling came to be.

What's a Widow to Do?

Another area where I felt guilt was in my parenting.

It had been some time since I defined myself as anything other than a married woman. The Lord knows that I was not the perfect wife. If you knew me before, you might not even recognize the upwardly mobile businesswoman I presented then to those on the outside. Oh, I gave God lots of lip service, but He was not the center of my life. I did many of the things that successful women do: I traveled, went to corporate parties and left my children to the care of my husband and my live-in housekeeper most of the time. After my husband died, I was still in a job that required more than forty hours a week and I could no longer afford a babysitter. My children were older now, my daughter, fifteen, and my son, eleven.

I think one of the worst parts of the early days of being a widow, for me, was recognizing how detached I was. In the first year, I ran away from my children emotionally. I remember going to a meeting and leaving Robert with my friend. My heart aches to think about it now. I could see that Robert wanted me to stay and I still left. I feel a hole in my gut every time I think of that night. Why couldn't I have just stayed and taken him to a movie or just watched TV with him? Even now, I wish I could get that first couple of years back. But I can't.

I remember one day, about a year after Phil died, I was finally cleaning out his closet. I found a box. I opened it and I found all the things I had missed from my daughter's childhood: her Girl Scout awards, pictures, red ribbons and school papers. There were pictures of field trips, horseback riding and report cards. There were pictures of her pet rabbits, Peaches and Snowball. I realized that so many of those events were lost and I sat on my bed crying.

She walked in and said, "What's wrong, Mom?"

I told her, "I found this box, in Dad's closet."

She replied, "I know, Mom, I miss him too."

I corrected her. "No Katy, I am not sad because of Dad. I am sad because of all the things I missed in your life because I was working so much."

She answered, "That's okay, Mom. Just be here now." And she hugged me.

Slowly I was waking up from a fog and there we were. I was then, first and foremost, a single mom. Phil was gone and it was up to me.

In 1999, I made the decision to move from our home to a smaller condominium. I thought I was doing the best thing to get Robert into a better high school and to reduce expenses. It turned out not to be such a great decision because he had a hard time leaving his friends and making new ones. For him it was just another loss. Even today I am saddened when I think of how lost and lonely he must have felt.

On the day of our move, someone new came into our lives. He often tells the story of how he met me. It was the day we were moving in 1999. Katy was so excited for me to meet this boy, Erik. She had so many boyfriends so I did not think much about it at the time. He was trying to make a good impression and I just told him to grab the end of a table and start helping us move; so much for being a sensitive mother. From the day I first met him, Erik and Katy were inseparable, until he left for the Air Force in 2000. I'm sure they still have a good laugh when they talk about the time I gave Erik "the father talk" about respecting Katy. I thought it was my job to try to intimidate him like a father might.

From the first week after Phil died, I spent a lot of time with a friend of Phil and we eventually became romantically involved. He was going through a divorce and we were both pretty broken. The relationship lasted about three years. I think this allowed me to postpone the grief in many ways. When the break up happened, it became a very complicated grief process and I needed professional help to get through it. It was his daughter that got me to go back to church. She is still a dear friend to me and we keep in touch.

I recall that in the spring of 2000, I began to have a very bad time when my three year relationship broke up and then both children graduated: Robert from junior high and Katy from high school. I was very depressed and called my sister, Nancy. I remember that she was very stern and said, "Those kids have missed too many opportunities for good memories. You need to get it together, get a cake, invite family and have a party to celebrate. Give them a good memory and you can cry tomorrow." I was so angry with her; I felt she did not understand. But she was right. And she came to the party along with other friends and family and we took pictures and we did not miss it.

I started back to school in the fall of 2000 to get my Master's in clinical psychology. The more I learned, the more aware I became of the needs of both of my children. I remember them rolling their eyes every time I called a family meeting and saying to me, "Do we really have to talk about feelings again?"

On September 11, 2001, the world changed for all of us; but for my little family, it would never be the same. My daughter left for the Air Force a week later. We went to her graduation from boot camp in San Antonio, Texas. I was so proud of her. My little girl had become a beautiful young woman. Six months later she married her high school sweetheart, Erik. When Erik asked me if he could marry Katy in January 2002, I was very worried because they were both not quite 20. But they were determined and married in April 2002.

Katy went on to be Airman of the Year at one of her bases. She completed her service and was honorably discharged in 2007.

Phil and I have grandchildren. I was privileged to be with Katy when she gave birth to Erin. Erik was in training out of state. I got the call that Katy was going into labor so I hopped on a redeye flight. I arrived at Denver Airport and drove through the night in the snow to Cheyenne, Wyoming. I got to be there to welcome our granddaughter, Erin, born on January 27, 2004. I got to stay with Katy and Erin for the first few weeks.

Erik served his country and his family, boots on the ground in Afghanistan in 2008. But he got to be there for the birth of my second grandson, Evan (named for his grandfather: Phillip Evan Connor), who was born November 2, 2009. They now live in the faith and have brought up their children in the faith. Katy completed nursing school and passed her examinations to be a registered nurse in August 2011.

I'm sure if you asked her, Katy would talk about her father not being there for so many important things: the last father-daughter dance her senior year, her graduation from boot camp, her wedding, the birth of her daughter and then her son and finally when she graduated nursing school and became an R.N. She would tell you that her life would have been very different if he were here. But I know that both of her fathers in heaven are as proud of her as I am.

My son, Robert, was only eleven when he lost his father. I am sad to admit that I was not there for him as I should have been at that time. I was very broken and distracted by a relationship that started too soon after Phil died. My brother tried to step in and be there for Robert. He took over coaching Robert's Little League team.

As he grew older, Robert became closed off. He avoided his time with my brother, Bill. His new friends were not the best influence. He began to act out, especially when his sister left for the Air Force in 2001. On the day of his sister's rehearsal dinner (in 2002), he became very upset. Katy came and got me out of the shower with shampoo still in my hair and said, "Something is wrong with Robert." He was very frightened because someone had threatened his life. Robert and I missed the rehearsal dinner but made it to the rehearsal with Katy worried, disappointed and upset. We ended up sending him away to live with family until after school was out. I took my comprehensive examinations about two weeks later. By the grace of God, I passed.

In the years to come, it became evident that Robert was struggling with a substance abuse problem. I recall one night I was living with my sister, Dori. Robert had graduated from one of his rehab programs and was supposed to be going to an AA convention. I had the number of his friend that he was supposed to meet. He lived all the way on the opposite side of Los Angeles. When I found out he never made it there, I was very worried because Robert had not been driving that long. Dori and I went looking for him and followed the route we thought he would have taken. Along the way, we saw a huge accident and the car was a small black car like Robert's. I was terrified. As we pulled up, we saw it was not his car, but there was another young man lying in the road. Dori and I never found him and eventually went back home. After calling the police to report him missing, I remember lying down at about three in the morning. I just prayed and gave him over to God. Within a few minutes I heard his key in the door. If I hadn't been so scared it would have been funny. He walked in as if nothing was wrong. I asked where he was and he said, "I told you, I went to the AA convention with my friend." I told him to wait and I went and got Dori up. I brought her in and said, "Dori, Robert is here and he said he was with his friend at the AA convention." Dori and I let him make up his whole story about how he was with that friend and everything they did. Then I asked him why his friend had been calling all night looking for him. This is just one of many stories from that difficult time. I never thought it would happen to my child.

His grandmother, my brother, Bill, and my sisters, Dori, Nancy, Elise and Kathy, were all supportive and tried to be helpful. Bill was very involved in attending Robert's recovery family groups and that relationship was eventually restored. Robert finally acknowledged that Bill was really like another father to him. Robert was finally able to share his resentments toward Katy and me.

Robert's turning point came when really I let go. I called my sister, Kathy and asked her to drive him to another free treatment facility in San Diego and told him I could do nothing more for him. She said that she thought this was a divine appointment for her and she was able to talk to Robert about the Lord. Within a few days I got a call that he had called her and told her that he accepted the Lord. She told me that he was afraid to call me because he thought I would not believe it or that he was trying to manipulate me. He was partly right because he had lied so often before.

I'd like to say that everything changed immediately, but as with most of us, the recovery was a process, not an event. After more than ten years and eleven different treatment programs (in-patient and outpatient), Robert graduated from college in 2015 with a degree in Geology. He also was able to develop a close relationship with his grandmother (Phil's mother) that is still a great blessing to her and him. He calls her about once a week just to talk. In addition to his uncle Bill, he developed close relationships with his uncle, Tim, my father and his uncle, Frank. It was very difficult for him when Frank died in 2009 and then when my father died in 2012, but he is still okay.

If you asked Robert, he might tell you that if his father had not died he would not have had to leave his friends in ninth grade. He would have graduated from a regular high school and played more sports. He might tell you that he would not have had to spend so much time with a depressed single mother or alone; and his father would be there for his graduations. He might tell you that he would not have been so angry. I recall that Phil said he was afraid Robert would be an angry young man and he wished he could say something to him to help, but he did not know what to say.

A short time ago I was having a down day. Robert came to me and said he wrote a song for me. I was speechless (something quite unusual for me). He put on some music and read it like a rap song. This is the song he wrote:

> Dear Mom
> After a night of reminiscing
> I decided to write this psalm
> After 27 years
> And thousands of tears you've carried me by your side...
> Even after Dad died
> You were always committed
> A single mother, please tell me how you did it.
> For that there's no way I would pay you back,
> But my plan is to show you that I understand...
> You are appreciated.
> Before our relationship becomes more belated,
> And I thank you for all the times you prayed for me,
> Because of all the times you were afraid for me.

Growing up I chose not to obey but rather "partay."
And even though I act crazy...
I have to thank the Lord that you made me.
You are appreciated for how you raised me
And all the extra love that you gave me.
You are appreciated.

I realize that many mothers, more worthy than I, never get to hear things like this from their children. But this was an unbelievable gift. The Bible says that the Lord "is a Father to the Fatherless, a defender of widows . . . God sets the lonely in families" (Ps. 68:5-6).

We will not know why we have to lose people we love, but we can depend on God because He can make good out of our sorrows. "I will turn their mourning into gladness; I will give them comfort and joy instead of sorrow"(Jeremiah 31:13). What an amazing gift He gave me the night my son gave me that poem. It is one of the highlights of my life.

By the grace of God, I became a licensed Marriage and Family therapist in June 2005. These days I get to work a lot with adults, families and couples. I do a lot of grief counseling.

This is my story and it is not over yet. This is how I cope: sometimes well, sometimes not so well. What I can tell you is that God is making something out of my story and more importantly, something out of me and those I love . . . and you. I don't believe He made cancer, war, murder, mental illness or child abuse. I don't believe God ever intended for us to be disabled, deformed, addicted, fat, injured or infirmed. He did not make us for death but for life. He designed us to live well with strong hearts, alert minds and pure spirits.

When I read the story of Job, I see that we are in the middle of a war between God and Satan. God is more powerful, more lovable and He knows the limits of our endurance.

I do believe He is constantly remaking us, comforting us and using us when we get hit in the crossfire. I also know that He can be trusted and He will make it right in the end.

So on your journey, I wish you more sweet grief than pain, I wish you many roses among the thorns, I wish you more prayers than cusswords and I wish you more happy endings than tragedies. Most of all, I wish you a good day until God and your loved ones welcome you at the finish line on your last day.

Diane

My first hint that things might go wrong came within moments after I dialed the phone.

I had been so eager to make the call. I had just received the letter in the mail telling me that I had been accepted to the hospital chaplain training program, which had been my heart's desire to attend. After serving as a volunteer chaplain at my church, I was finally going to train for a professional career as a healthcare chaplain. I was over the moon with excitement. I quickly called the number listed in the letter to set up an appointment with my assigned trainer.

As my trainer told me where I was assigned, my heart started beating a little faster. I would be working at Norris Cancer Center in Los Angeles. "Do you have any problems with your assignment?" my trainer had asked.

I had never worked with cancer patients. I took a deep breath as I quickly assured myself that I would soon be learning the skills I didn't yet possess. "No, it's fine," I had assured my trainer, with far more confidence in my voice than I felt in my heart.

Once the call was completed, I looked up the Norris Cancer Center address. Once again, I drew in a breath as I noticed that it was in a part of L.A. I seldom traveled. Like many residents of Los Angeles suburbs, I tried to stay out of downtown Los Angeles unless it was absolutely necessary to brave the mind numbing traffic.

I drove nervously on my first trip to Norris. I had trouble finding a parking spot so I circled around until I found a vacancy—next to a temporary outbuilding that was marked County Morgue. As I exited my car, I paused as a man in hospital garb pushed a gurney across my path as he entered the building. A covered body lay on the gurney.

Unsure where to go and a little unnerved by what I had just seen, I wandered the huge campus until I saw a gathering of people. They were lined up, waiting for something. I also saw two armed guards, keeping the people under control. Timidly, I approached one of the guards, eying the pistol in his holster. "You have to get in line for your meds, just like all the other psychiatric patients," he said gruffly. "Go on, over there. " He pointed to the end of the line.

"No," I protested. "I'm trying to find the chaplain's office."

He looked as if he didn't believe me, but then pointed at a door. "You have to go through the psych ward. Give me your I.D. and I'll unlock the door for you."

At that point I did something I'm not proud of. The tense drive through the heavy L.A. traffic, the body on the gurney, the armed guard, the psychiatric patients, the locked door and the yet unacknowledged fear of working with cancer patients, all overcome me. "That's O.K.," I said. "I'll come back later." I turned and fled to my car as quickly as I could. Once inside, I called my trainer and told him I couldn't make our meeting. The truth was, though, I didn't want to make the meeting. I simply didn't want to be at Norris Cancer Center.

Not all situations are so easy to run away from though. Sometimes we have no choice but to stay.

The first time I learned this principle, I was a fourteen-year-old Girl Scout, stuck at the bottom of the Grand Canyon.

My troop had decided to take a raft trip, running what should have been easy rapids. What we didn't know was that unexpected weather conditions had turned those rapids from the gentle thrill ride we expected into a potentially life threatening torrent. The solemn look on our professional and experienced guide's face said more than his words as he explained the risk we were about to face. The steep walls of the Canyon hemmed us in. There was no land we could clamor on to and portage around the rapids. Neither was there any landing spot where a helicopter could airlift frightened girls off the river. If we ever wanted to see our homes again, we had to go through the rapids.

"What are we going to do?" one girl had asked in a quavering voice, voicing the fear we all felt. None of us wanted to go through that roaring rapid. Joyce, our adult leader, answered her by softly breaking into song.

"Rock my soul in the bosom of Abraham, rock my soul in the bosom of Abraham, rock my soul in the bosom of Abraham, oh, rock-a my soul," she sang. Then she moved into the verse, changing the words to match our circumstances. "So high, I can't get over it, so low, I can't get under it, so wide, I can't get 'round it, gotta go through that rapid."

I had never heard the words to "Rock My Soul in the Bosom of Abraham" before, but they quickly seared their way into my soul.

Still, as she sang, I pictured myself snuggly cuddled in God's lap, His loving Presence protecting me from harm. I held on to that image as I wrapped my hands around the raft's ropes, holding on tightly so I wouldn't be washed downriver if we capsized in the roaring water. Soon we were all singing along with Joyce.

Whether it was due to our guide's exceptional river running skill or the grace of God, we all made it safely through that rapid and emerged into calmer water, with the raft still upright and all us girls intact.

I never forgot the song. In fact, it was that song that floated into my mind on another day when I faced treacherous circumstances.

One evening, as I stood in front of a crowd of people, chairing a meeting at church, I suddenly I felt a searing pain in my abdomen. I tried to ignore it and concentrate on the meeting, but the pain kept growing. I brought the meeting to a close as quickly as I could and rushed to my car. I thought that if I got home and lay down, I'd feel better.

Once home, the pain continued to grow. Realizing I was in trouble, I asked my teenaged son to drive me to the emergency room of a local hospital.

At the hospital, I sat in the emergency room for nearly three hours, waiting to be seen and wondering how much pain I could stand before I lost consciousness. A nurse finally called me and I began answering insistent questions and was sent off to the ultrasound and then to the CT scan machine. Eventually, I was told that I had a mass in my abdomen, probably a large ovarian cyst and it looked like my left ovary had ruptured. No wonder it hurt so badly! They gave me some pain medication and sent me home to wait for the surgery they had scheduled for a few days later.

The next day I saw a surgeon. He did a CA-125 blood test to check for ovarian cancer. Later he told me that the test was negative. There was no evidence of ovarian cancer.

I underwent a laparoscopic surgery a few days later. I recovered well enough to attend my oldest son's wedding eleven days after my operation.

I also recovered well enough to continue my graduate studies. In spite of my false start at Norris Cancer Center years earlier, I had regained enough nerve to enroll in professional theological studies at a local seminary.

A year and a half later, I again developed a presumed ovarian cyst, this time in my right ovary, which was large enough to cause persistent pain. Again, a CA-125 test came back showing no sign of cancer. The day my youngest son graduated from high school, I underwent my second laparoscopic surgery. I didn't make it to his graduation ceremony.

But I did make it to my own graduation the following year. I had completed my seminary studies and landed a job as a hospice chaplain. I finally got the training I had run from at Norris.

Although I cherished my days in hospice, it wasn't long before an even more exciting job opened up for me. My home church hired me to serve as the Care Pastor. This enabled me to serve the needs of about 3000 attendees and to train others to work as prayer and care volunteers. It was truly my dream job. I planned to work at that job until I was forced to retire.

But life seemed to have other plans in store for me. About a year later I noticed a persistent dull pain in my belly. My stomach felt bloated all the time and I was perpetually tired, even after a good night's rest. I mentioned these things to my family doctor. He told me it was nothing serious, probably irritable bowel syndrome and that I should just ignore the situation. I tried to follow his advice, but the pain became more insistent. I made an appointment with the surgeon who had done my previous two surgeries to see what he thought.

After another ultrasound, this doctor, an ob-gyn, told me I had another pelvic mass. Another CA-125 assured us that it wasn't ovarian cancer. But, since the mass was causing pain, it needed to go. This time, he would do a hysterectomy in order to remove the mass. And no, I couldn't have a laparoscopic procedure this time.

As I sat in the doctor's office, alone, without anyone by my side, I felt overwhelmed with fear. I knew I needed another surgery and that it would be more extensive than the last two procedures, but I couldn't make myself walk through that door just yet. I left the doctor's office, telling him I needed to check my work schedule before I consented to a surgery date.

The next morning I received a telephone call from the police department in the town where my brother, my only sibling, lived. He had been found, dead, in his car. Suddenly I had to quickly fly cross country to "dispose of the remains" and settle my brother's estate.

By the time I finished wrapping up my brother's final business and making arrangements for what needed to be done at work while I took a medical leave, nearly two months had passed since I had been told I needed surgery. By this time my physical pain was so intense that I was almost glad to enter the hospital.

Not only was my physical condition preparing me for surgery, but I was also being emotionally and spiritually prepared also, even though I didn't realize it at the time. In my journal there are two entries from about a week before surgery.

Monday, March 14, 2005

There are many thoughts in my head and heart so even though I haven't journaled for quite a while, it seems wise to give them a place to roam unfettered.

I've been waiting for surgery for some time now. Part of me is actually looking forward to the surgery. I want to be on the other side of it. I want to be at the place where I say, "Wow, it's been a week, a month, a year since surgery." I want to start rebuilding my life. And yet, this time is valuable too. This is my life just as much as the time after surgery.

Lord, please help me to accomplish your will in this waiting time as well as in the time after.

I feel some fear about surgery but mostly I feel trust. Trust in the Lord to keep me safe. Trust that things will go well. Part of me wants to simply lie back and let what happens, happen. Part of me even believes that the surgery is exactly what God has preordained for my life, even before I was born. I believe He has been drawing me to this moment, setting all the elements in place, carefully preparing each detail of the event. How weird is that!

And yet, I need to let myself voice the fear also.

I'm feeling a bit more anxiety about Monday. I talked to my husband about organ donating if things go wrong. I told him to go ahead and agree to donate if someone asks him about a specific, immediate need. I've never felt comfortable with that for but today, I did.

I've had several thoughts about the timing of the surgery. Spring begins tomorrow. A time of new birth, of renewal, cleansing, freshness and growth. Spring cleaning—out with the old, the tired, the useless. In my case, it's even spring cleaning for my body.

Tomorrow is also the beginning of Holy Week. I find parallels with Jesus' last week in my surgery. I'm allowing someone to hurt me, to put me in a deathlike state for a higher purpose—to accomplish healing. In a way, I'm looking at my time in the hospital as analogous to Jesus's time in the grave.

But after death, comes resurrection. New life! A transformed life.

I don't know what my new life will be, but I'm looking forward to it. I'm hoping my death experience (surgery, anesthesia, hospitalization) will somehow benefit others beyond me (as well as me).

Although my first two surgeries had helped reduce my anxiety before the third and had helped to build my trust that the Lord would get me through this tough circumstance, there was no way they could have readied me for the results of surgery number three.

When the day arrived and the surgeon finally opened me up and laid eyes on the troublesome abdominal mass, he didn't like what he saw. He called another doctor into the operating room to give his opinion. The other doctor knew immediately what it was. They did a quick biopsy and collected tissue samples for further analysis.

Sometime after he stitched me up, my surgeon came to the recovery room where I had been wheeled to groggily fight my way back into awareness. He stood by my side and delivered the words that would change my world forever. "Cancer," he said. "We found cancer. And we weren't able to remove it all."

"Rock'a my soul in the bosom of Abraham," floated into my still drugged brain. "Gotta go through that rapid," played in my head as I sank back into unconsciousness.

A few hours later, when my head began to clear from the anesthesia, my family reiterated what the surgeon had said. In spite of the good results on the pre-operative CA-125 test, I did indeed have some kind of ovarian cancer.

That night, alone in my hospital bed, I felt incredibly alone and frightened. What would become of me? Was I going to die? What kinds of torturous treatments would I have to undergo? The tears trickled down my cheeks just as a nurse entered the room. Taking a look at my face she said, "Oh, honey, just relax."

"How can I relax?" I said, with a touch of bitterness in my voice. "I just learned that I have cancer."

"You concentrate on getting through the next minute and then the next one and the next one. One minute at a time. You don't try to figure it all out at once. Right now you are safe in your bed, being looked after. Think about that," she said.

If I could have snorted in derision at her simplistic words without hurting my stitches, I would have. "She doesn't understand," I thought.

But after she left, I did think about her words. For the moment I was okay. And maybe that was enough.

The next day a Eucharistic minister came to give communion to my Catholic roommate. I eavesdropped as the minister said, "Be thankful that you have been chosen to share in the suffering of Jesus. Not everyone gets that privilege." Again, I wanted to shout, "You don't get it! Nobody wants to suffer. It is not a privilege!" But I didn't. It would have hurt too much. Instead I quietly begged the Lord to help me get through this.

Getting through my cancer diagnosis involved so much more than physical treatment and recovery.

Although the hospital released me a few days after my surgery, my cancer journey had just begun. My surgeon sent samples of the tumor he had removed to a tumor registry across the country. We had to wait several days to find out from them just exactly what type of ovarian cancer I had. Then we had to find an oncologist. My surgeon's office searched for facilities that would take my insurance, be appropriate for me and be willing to take my care. Then they called me with their findings.

"Mrs. Fillmore," the nurse said. "We have your results back from the tumor board and we have located two oncologists. Which one would you like to make an appointment with?"

The nurse rattled off two facility names. The first location had recently suffered some bad publicity in the media. The second was the University of Southern California. Since I was wary of the first facility and figured that a large university would be equipped to handle rare cases, as mine was, I chose USC.

It wasn't until the fog from my pain medications lifted that I realized I was about to become a patient at Norris Cancer Center, the oncology branch of the University of Southern California Medical Center and the same place I had run away from several years prior.

Later I journaled about becoming a Norris patient.

April 3, 2005

I went to church today for the first time since December. It felt so good to be part of the worshiping community. While at church I had one of those moments where you "hear" that voice within. It had to do with a commissioning service that was held right before I graduated from seminary about four years previous. This is what I heard, approximately:

"Remember your commissioning service at Azusa Pacific? Remember how the ministry opportunities kept opening to you after you publically declared your commitment to serve Me?

You have never left that service. You have simply been on various assignments. What you are going through now is no different. It is simply another assignment. You have completed your other assignments and now I'm moving you on to another task.

Remember how I sent my Son to minister to humankind? Remember how He had to become human in order to minister to humans? So I am sending you. To minister to cancer patients. To bring My hope where there is no hope. But, just like My Son, in order to minister to cancer patients, you must become one. You need to be inside the world participating in it, in order to reach it.

I have been preparing you for this all your life. I even created your body so that it could have the cancer that would bring you to this place in your life."

This is the gist of what I heard. I don't especially like it. I've just recorded it.

In spite of these inspiring words, I struggled with my new identity as a cancer patient. I had always been a person who derived her sense of value from the thing she did. My self-worth was tied to the number of items checked off my "to do" list at the end of the day. And here I was, only slightly more able to care for myself than a newborn. Just walking to the bathroom exhausted me. I knew that eventually I would regain strength, but I struggled with feeling worthless since I couldn't be up doing things for others.

And then there was my job, my dream position that fulfilled my lifelong desire to be a professional minister. In the midst of all of my physical illness, I had quit my job. I didn't know what my upcoming treatment would entail or even if I'd live and since I didn't want my congregation to suffer because my sick body wouldn't allow me to provide the quality pastoral care I wanted to, I had resigned, leaving room for a healthy minister to take over the position. But so much of my sense of self had been wrapped up in that job. Who was I now that I wasn't a pastor? I felt lost and purposeless.

My first visit with my Norris Cancer Center oncologist went well. She felt that my cancer had been adequately treated by the surgery. "Of course, if the cancer returns, it will lower your odds of survival," she added. "But we will deal with that if the time comes."

Since at that time there was no evidence that my particular brand of cancer would even respond to radiation or chemo, the doctor decided simply to give me frequent checkups and do nothing else at that moment.

I returned from that visit optimistic about my chances of survival. As soon as I was able, I returned to caring for my family, making sure to include lots of rest time into my schedule. My unemployed state came in handy as my father's Alzheimer's worsened and my mother needed more help in caring for him. Since I wasn't working, I could be there for both my parents. Although I still felt purposeless without my job, the busyness of daily life kept me from falling too deeply into the pit of depression.

About nine months after my cancer diagnosis, a checkup with my oncologist brought more bad news. During the physical exam she had felt another mass. She sent me for an ultrasound and a P. E. T. scan. Both tests confirmed her suspicions that a mass had returned. She recommended another surgery, this time at USC.

The surgery was scheduled for late February, but a week before the date, I caught the flu and had to reschedule. In early March, my father complained of severe stomach pain I took him to the doctor who then promptly sent him to the emergency room, where he was hospitalized for an aortic aneurysm. He died on April 3rd. I was so thankful that I wasn't recovering from surgery and was able to be there for my parents at this crucial time. Sometimes, things like the flu can work in our favor.

I finally had my surgery on June 1. The surgery was as surprising as the last, only with a twist. In my last surgery I had gone under the knife believing myself to be cancer free, only to discover I had cancer. In the surgery I had expected more cancer, but got different results. To my surgeon's surprise, there was no trace of the tumor that had appeared in the ultrasound and P.E. T. scan. None. No cancer present. What an unexpected gift!

Once I recovered from surgery, I eased back into life. Unfortunately, the surgery had left me with an incisional hernia, so I had to adjust to a gentler way of life, with minimal lifting. Still, I helped my mother adjust to widowhood, taking her on trips and eventually helping her move into a retirement community where she could live a more active life. I did some volunteer work, always keeping my need for a well-rested and balanced schedule in view. I still missed my job, but found I didn't have enough physical energy to return to work.

That lack of energy turned out to be a good thing because my mother's health soon took a nosedive. A previous bout with breast cancer reoccurred, this time with the cancer having spread into her hip bones. Once again, my unemployed state (due to my own health problems) allowed me the time to care for my mother in her final days.

One crucial aspect of this time was that my mother had never expressed her faith in Jesus Christ as her Savior, a vital step for everyone, but especially so for a person facing imminent death. While I had accepted God's plan of salvation as a teenager, my mother had staunchly resisted my efforts to discuss "religion" with her. I respected her wishes but continued to pour out Christ's love on her as I cared for her needs. I believe this opportunity to serve her in this quiet way helped soften her heart. The evening before one of her cancer surgeries, I asked her if she knew what would happen to her if her weak heart didn't make it through the surgery. She asked me how she could be sure of her destiny. I told her of her need to accept Jesus as your Savior and, for the first time in her life, she expressed belief in Christ's salvation.

When I left my mom's hospital room that night, I knew that not only had I witnessed a miracle—an 80-year-old woman being born anew—but also that I had fulfilled one of the tasks for which I had been created. I had long suspected that I, as an adoptee, had been placed into my adoptive family so that one day I could help my family find eternal life. I had previously shared special spiritual experiences with both my brother and my father before their deaths. My mother had been the last "hold-out." But on that night, I believe my task had been completed within my adoptive family. And I also believe that my being able to spend quality time with my family due to the cancer that sidelined me from my busy career oriented life may have contributed to this outcome.

The next period of time was really rough emotionally. Although I was only in my mid 50's now, my entire family of origin had died and I felt intensely lonely. My husband's congenital disability, previously mild, had progressed so that he was no longer able to work and was in need of a full time caregiver. My oldest son and his family moved across the country for his job, taking our grandchildren, whom we had babysat often, away. My husband's mother was showing increasing signs of dementia so we moved her to a care facility near us and I took on the responsibility of overseeing her care.

My oncologist had warned me that stress might be a factor in cancer recurrence. It turned out that she was right, at least for me. All the emotions of death and family change took their toll on me. It wasn't long before my doctor found another mass, which meant that technically this was now the third time my cancer had occurred. I prepared to undergo surgery yet again.

Since I was already going to be under anesthesia, I decided to take advantage of the situation and ask my surgeon if she could repair the incisional hernia that had occurred after the last surgery. She agreed, noting that I would have to stay at least an extra day in the hospital to allow for extra recovery time.

Once again, I had cancer surgery at USC Medical Center.

Surgery recovery is never pleasant and this time was no exception. This time I noted that the pain medication seemed to interfere with my sense of time. I remember looking at the clock and then closing my eyes. I would open my eyes again, thinking that an hour must have elapsed, only to find that only a minute had passed. This altered sense of time made my four day hospital stay feel like four weeks.

The day before I was due to go home, I decided to take a walk down the hall. I have learned that walking after surgery helps me recover quicker. So, no matter how much it hurts, I force myself to walk after operations. Grabbing my I.V. pole, I hobbled into the hallway. I took a few steps down the hall and noticed another patient out for a "stroll."

"Wanna race?" she said.

I laughed as much as the forty-three staples in my abdomen would allow. "Wha'cha in for?" I countered. "Armed robbery? Grand theft auto?"

She smiled. Her surgery was more recent than mine so she was not up to laughing yet. "Nope, ovarian cancer. They just found it." Anxiety flitted across her face. "I don't know what will happen next."

"Been there, done that," I offered. " I'm on my third go round."

"Your third bout with cancer? Aren't you scared?" Her question reflected her own terror.

I thought for a moment and then honestly replied. "No, not really. I've had a lot of time to thrash through my feelings. It really helps to know that I have a loving Heavenly Father who takes good care of me. I have complete confidence that regardless of what happens to my body, I know that I am going to be okay. There is a lot to look forward to in heaven, if God decides to take me."

Her eyes widened. "You look so calm. I wish I could believe in God like that!"

"Why can't you?" I probed as gently as I could.

"Well, I had a father who abused me. It is hard to believe in a loving Heavenly Father when your earthly father is a monster. He not only robbed me of my childhood, he also robbed me of my ability to have faith." Her eyes glistened with tears.

"I read once that there is a correlation between sexual abuse and cancer. A lot of us are in the same boat with you."

"You too?" she asked.

I nodded. Although someone other than my father had been my abuser, I had struggled for years with unpleasant memories. I had also spent years in counseling to reach the point where I could honestly say what I said next. "But, you know, it helps to know that no matter how bad our earthly families were, God is not like that. He is the perfect, loving Father we all long for. His plan is for our welfare, even when it doesn't feel like it."

I thought about all the blessings that had come to me as a result of my cancer struggles. "We often go through lots of pain in our lives, but it is not without a purpose. Sometimes we suffer because God is using the bad to shape us into the loving people He wants us to be.

As I spoke, I could feel strength and love pouring out of me towards her. She stood looking at me, as if weighing every word I'd said.

"You give me such hope," she said finally. "I didn't think that someone who had been abused and who had cancer could believe in God. It is so wonderful to know that it is possible."

"I think God allowed me to be here today, just so you could see how much healing He can provide."

"Do you think He'd do that for me?" The longing to know such a loving God poured out of her.

"He just did."

The tears trickled down her face. I asked if I could pray for her and she eagerly agreed. I took her hand and she squeezed it warmly.

"Dear Heavenly Father," I prayed aloud. "Please help this beloved child of Yours know how much You love her. Give her hope in the midst of this rough time. Grant her the faith she desires."

"Thank you," she murmured. "Thank you."

As I raised my bowed head I saw a nurse standing near us. "Time to take your vitals," she said.

Obediently we both hobbled back to our rooms. We were, after all, both recovering from major surgery.

I felt exhausted when I returned to bed; exhausted, but happy. As I lay in bed, savoring the chance the rest, I heard a voice in my head. "That's why you were here. That's why I brought you to this hospital at this time. For her."

A deep wave of satisfaction washed over me, leaving tears of joy in my eyes. *I think I just completed another of the tasks I was created for. Thank you, Lord. I'm glad I came.*

The fact that I am writing this story four years after my third bout with cancer will let you know that I survived. I did undergo pelvic radiation after surgery though and that was hard. Although not everyone has intense side effects from such treatment, I did. But those radiation days gave me another chance to practice trusting and believing in the goodness of God, even when it was hard to do so. "Rock my soul in the bosom of Abraham" was often on my lips as I lay on the table, underneath the huge radiation machine, allowing it to damage my body so that I might eventually heal.

I had another opportunity to trust about a year after my third cancer surgery. This time the oncologist found that I had thyroid nodules. I once again wanted to run away when the doctor recommended a biopsy. I hate needles and the thought of having someone jab them into my throat, while I was awake, sent me crying out to God, asking Him why I had to undergo yet another unpleasant procedure. The biopsy turned out to be not nearly as bad as my fears of it though and while the test results showed infection, there was no trace of cancer.

About a year later I learned the reason behind my little thyroid scare.

A friend who lives about 500 miles from me had noticed an article in her newspaper about a registry for ovarian cancer patients. The registry was looking for patients who had a particular rare type of cancer because researchers had discovered a possible genetic cause behind the cancer.

I called the research center to find out if I qualified for their study. They were interested in the type of cancer I'd had AND the fact that I had thyroid nodules. Apparently, having both signaled that I might have the genetic mutation they were seeking to study.

Subsequently, I sent samples of my DNA to a National Institute of Health Facility in Maryland. Over the next few weeks I spoke with a genetic counselor who told me that some new and exciting studies were being conducted which focused on a previously unknown mechanism by which cancer develops. By studying cases like mine, researchers planned to develop new treatments and possibly even cures for some types of cancer.

Initially, I had mixed feelings about participating in the study. I had to journal about my feelings and present them to God in prayer. Who wants to be known for their genetic mutation? It took several days of mulling over the possibilities and asking God to give me insight into the situation, before I could feel at ease with my situation.

Gradually I began to realize that if my cancer was due to a genetic mutation then that meant I had been created in the womb with the ability to develop my particular brand of cancer. But why would a loving God do such a thing to an innocent fetus? Perhaps it was because He knew that fetus would grow into a woman who loved Him and wanted to serve Him. Perhaps it was because He knew that He was also filling the woman with a desire to serve her fellow humans and that this was the way that would best allow her to satisfy that desire. Perhaps He was equipping her very body to carry out the tasks He had planned, even before she was born, for her to accomplish in her lifetime.

As I prayed, I started to feel that familiar rush of deep joy that comes from sensing that God has a purpose for you and that you are cooperating with Him in accomplishing it. I stopped feeling anxious about the research study and instead was overwhelmed with gratitude. I suddenly felt that it was a gift to be granted cancer. It was a way I could potentially be part of saving many other families in the future from undergoing the same suffering I had. It was a way to contribute to the welfare of humankind. I felt deeply humbled to be given the sacred opportunity to help in this highly personal way.

ဆာ๛

Today, I am doing well. My body bears scars and weaknesses but my soul is well. I've learned so much from my cancer suffering. Some of the things I've come to know are:

- That sometimes the experiences we resist the most are the very ones we and others around us, most need.
- That it is possible to find peace in the midst of a storm.
- That God does not inflict pain on His children randomly. He has a sacred purpose for the trials He allows in our lives.
- That cooperating with God in what He wants to do in our lives brings deep, lasting, soul satisfying joy, even when it hurts.

Looking back over my first cowardly visit to Norris Cancer Center, when I ran away because I didn't want to go there, I know that even though I wouldn't have chosen all the suffering I endured over the past decade, I'm so glad God took me on the journey.

About the Authors

Nancy Brandon, the founder and organizer of *Sacred Suffering* lives in Yorba Linda, California with her beloved husband, Tim. She especially enjoys spending time with her family, each a special and unique blessing from the Lord.

A wife for almost 40 years, mother of six adult children, grandmother of nine, Nancy Brandon went back to school at the age of 50. While earning a bachelor degree in psychology at Biola she was diagnosed with ovarian cancer. After surgery and treatment she had a four and a half year remission, during which time she began a Master's degree program in Spiritual Direction and Soul Care at Talbot Seminary. During her graduate studies Nancy experienced the first of five cancer recurrences that have required four surgeries, chemos and radiation.

Nancy has led multiple spiritual direction groups, Bible studies and a cancer support group and has a special passion to minister to other cancer patients.

God's love, grace and kindness continue to carry her through the ongoing cancer journey as she learns to realize and embrace His faithful presence.

Trish Waltz recently moved from California and purchased a country home in Arkansas and resides with her husband and youngest son. Being a therapist for nearly three decades has brought her much joy. The greatest joy in her career was co-founding SPARE Ministries and Counseling Center, where she was the Executive Director and Clinical Supervisor for over ten years.

Trish enjoys the beauty of nature and is now exploring the beautiful Ozark Mountains whenever she has spare time. She is also learning to can all of the wonderful organic fruits and vegetables her husband is growing on their developing garden.

Ana Kikerpill lives in Southern California with her husband and best friend, Carl. They have a blended family of four daughters ranging in age from 14 to 29. She is a real estate agent who is currently enrolled in the Vineyard Community Church's Kingdom School of Ministry and works alongside her husband in their "Free to Love Again" Divorce Recovery Worskshops ministry. One of her passions is to give hope to and mentor single women who desire to be married.

Sharon Barnes and her husband, Paul, currently live in Southern California. Her life is full of joy with two great sons, a wonderful daughter-in-law and four active grandchildren by whom she is affectionately called, "Yomo", which is African for grandma.

Sharon has been involved in several ministry and work endeavors. She served as the Director of Ministry for New Life Ministries for twenty-five years where she helped to launch their national women's conferences, Women of Faith and then later presided over their coaching program and a nationwide network of over one thousand mental health counselors. She also functioned for seven years as the Regional Prayer Coordinator over seven counties in Southern California for the National Day of Prayer Task Force supporting county coordinators in their prayer efforts for their cities and nation.

Her continued passion is to help people become more aware of the love of Jesus and experience His power in their lives. Weaving her aspiration and life's mission together, Sharon recently founded Haven of Healing Ministry in 2014 to bring healing and encouragement to others through prayer, pastoral care and support. In addition, she currently functions as the Executive Director of Spare Counseling.

Diana Carver lived in Yorba Linda with her devoted husband, Rick Carver and their three children. When she wasn't wrangling their two very co-dependent dogs and one cat, she worked with her husband at his privately owned business. After her third and final diagnosis with cancer, Diana devoted her time to reaching out to her fellow cancer patients with the word of God, teaching them that they were not alone, that He was with them in all things.

Amanda Carver graduated from UC Santa Cruz and now works for her father at his business. It is her dream to one day become a renowned author.

Jane Smith (in keeping with the principles of her support organization, this is not her real name) lives in Southern California with her husband of eight years. She works a full-time job in commercial property management on the business campus where she and her husband met. Other than enjoying time with their family, Jane revels in the joy of dancing with her local ballet company performing classical ballet, modern and flamenco.

Lisa Patterson lives in Ontario, California with her husband and best friend, Gary. Together, they have raised seven sons and now are enjoying grandsons.

Lisa is the Director of Elementary Children's program at Purpose Church in Pomona. She is also the director of Recovery Ministries and serves as the ministry leader for Celebrate Recovery. She loves speaking and she serves as a Regional Speaker Trainer for Stonecroft Ministries.

Lisa considers her life a gift from God and believes this life is an adventure that is fully worth taking. Though she has endured some very painful things, she has discovered that Jesus is the One who is writing her story and everything she experiences has all been part of a greater plan, a plan that glorifies God and brings others to Him.

Cherie Francis-Boegeman is a pediatric occupational therapist and small business owner. She works with children diagnosed with autism and sensory integrative dysfunction at her clinic "The Launchpad, Therapy for Kids" in San Juan Capistrano, California. She is a speaker and co-founder of the "Free to Love Again" Divorce Recovery Workshop established in 2007. Cherie is also a speaker for "Elevated to Excellence, speaking to the value of every person...." She lives with her husband Steve and together they are parenting their 23 year-old daughter and 17 year-old son in Lake Forest, California. When not serving at The Connection Church of Orange County or on the sideline at the soccer field, Cherie enjoys hiking and camping.

Adrian Tremblay has a passion for Christ and lives to tell others what He has done in her life. She loves to read and study her Bible and has attended many Bible studies through the years. Adrian and her husband, Brian, reside in Orange County, California with her father. They have been blessed to attend Yorba Linda Friends Church for many years and have been involved in many different ministries.

At this time in Adrian's life her focus is giving care to her father and husband. Her five grandchildren bring her more love and joy than she could have ever imagined.

Tamra Hollar, known as Tami by her family and friends, is a Southern California native who lives in Whittier with her husband of nearly 44 years, Everett. Her two sons and their lovely wives live close by in neighboring cities. She loves spending time with her two beautiful grandchildren. She currently sings in the choir and serves as a deacon in her church. In recent years, God has given her a heart of compassion for the persecuted church and for several years now she has led a monthly women's meeting of intercessory prayer on their behalf. In her free time, Tami likes to quilt, garden and read.

Kathleen Hernandez is a Marriage & Family Therapist Intern at SPARE Counseling in Anaheim, California where her focus is on children, families and adults struggling with anxiety, grief and/or depression. She completed her Master of Science in Clinical Psychology at Vanguard University in 2012. Kathleen currently lives in Yorba Linda, California, with her husband. God, then her family, are what are most important to her.

Gloriann Connor is a Licensed Marriage and Family Therapist who lives in San Diego, California. After her husband died in 1997 she went back to school to become a therapist. She has been licensed for ten years, working with individuals, couples and families. She has worked alongside several churches and Christian ministries over the years: she began in 1999 working with Pomona First Baptist leading a Grief Ministry, a Post Abortion Ministry and eventually a recovery group ministry called Potter's Hands. She graduated with her Master of Arts in Marriage and Family therapy in 2002 at the age of 48. She moved to Barstow and built counseling relationships with New Life Fellowship in Barstow, First Methodist Church in Barstow and New Life Chapel in Hesperia. She worked with SPARE Ministries and then with Lutheran Social Services providing counseling for individuals, children and families. She has also worked as a facilitator with the New Life Ministries "Healing is a Choice." She has spent the last five years working with military service members and their families. She has two grown children and three grandchildren and a dog named Buddy.

Diane Fillmore lives in Southern California with her husband, Tom. A life-writing instructor and former chaplain and care pastor, she is currently in graduate school, training as a spiritual director. In her spare time she enjoys spending time with her family which includes two adult sons, a delightful daughter-in-law and three (incredibly adorable) grandchildren. One of her greatest joys is sharing the character of God with people and helping them see how He works in people's lives.

Topic Index

Also by Proclaim Press

"Why, Lord, why?" This is the pleading question of many diagnosed with cancer. Suzanne, diagnosed with cancer in her 30s, also heard her sons' questions. "Mama, what is cancer?" "Mama, can I hug you?" "Mama, will you die?" *Consider the Butterfly, Emerging from the Cancer Chrysalis* is a heartfelt cancer story written by an ordinary woman who experiences extraordinary miracles. This book takes the reader on a transformational walk with God through thought-provoking questions, inspirational scriptures and personal stories of transformation. You will learn how you can emerge from the "cancer chrysalis" of hopelessness, fear and despair to experience God's majesty in your life. Suzanne's testimony is an invaluable tool for all those who have struggled with major illness as well as for their family and friends.

25808550R10107

Made in the USA
San Bernardino, CA
13 November 2015